*Step into a delicious world
of Baileys treats ...*

The Baileys
COOKBOOK

HarperCollins*Publishers*

CONTENTS

INTRODUCTION

Come on in to the delicious world of Baileys!

If you've been looking for more indulgence, deliciousness, joy and mouth-watering-ness (it's a word) in your life, then you've picked the right book.

You're going to find page after page of sumptuous, yummy Baileys delights – martinis and mudslides, panna cotta and profiteroles – prepping you for everything from a casual Saturday brunch at a table filled with flowers and friends, to a huge birthday bash with lights, music, balloons and a bar. Hell, yeah – you deserve it.

Every recipe is one we want you to have as a reminder that life is for seizing, for enjoying, for sharing and for indulging. That every night is made for dancing and doughnuts, for karaoke and cocktails, and every season is good for indulgent stuffed Baileys pancake mornings and scrumptiously warming Baileys crumble and custard evenings.

Life is always worth enjoying – and if you're going to do it, you might as well do it deliciously.

xx

We're not just a globally beloved drink. We're a co-conspirator in the pursuit of pleasure.

OUR START

We were born in Ireland, in 1974, created by a small group of irrepressible characters who saw that times and tastes were changing, and that people wanted something new and indulgent. Pleasure was no longer something that required permission – it was there for anyone who knew where to look.

The group set out to craft an indulgent drink. Their mission was seemingly simple – to craft a perfect blend of two of Ireland's most indulgently delicious ingredients: rich, dairy cream and the finest whiskey.

They were told it was impossible, that those two ingredients would never stick. But they refused to give up. They'd let nothing stand in the way of their pursuit of delight.

It took them more than two years, but finally they had a breakthrough and brought these partners together in a rich, rewarding combination.

OUR COWS

Every year, 200 million litres of fresh Irish milk are required to produce the creamiest of cream used in the making of Baileys. This milk is supplied by cows we truly love on small, family-owned farms.

We're talking farms where the cows roam free in luscious green fields handed down from one generation to the next, grazing for roughly 200 days of the year and only coming inside in chilly weather. That's the secret to the deliciousness in every bottle.

OUR CRAFT

This unique concoction became an overnight sensation and today is voted the most-loved liquid in the world, with over 156 million people around the world enjoying Baileys. And the inventive passion and playful spirit in which it was created remains at the heart of everything we do, from embracing those who live life on their own terms, to creating year-round scrumptious recipes.

Over the last 40 years we've travelled the globe and are now sold in over 150 countries. But we've never forgotten our roots. To this day, every single bottle of Baileys Original is made in Ireland.

There's something deeply delicious in that liquid. Maybe it's the irrepressible Irish spirit. Maybe it's the passion of that original team, and their drive to create something more than a liqueur. Maybe it's the pleasure of a drink that says you can have it all.

Whatever it is, it's irresistible.

COCKTAIL KIT

While every cocktail in this book is delicious, it's also mind-blowing when the drink comes to the table (or sofa, picnic blanket or kitchen counter) and it looks so good that your mouth starts watering before you've even had the first sip. The glint of ice in the liquid, the bright freshness of the fruit or the delectable dripping chocolate sauce on the rim: each little extra turns a simple adult drink into a totally delish treat.

But that doesn't mean you have to borrow the finest crystal and silver drinkware. A Baileys cocktail is about fun right now, so if you don't have fancy balloon glasses, could you dress up normal glasses with a paper parasol and a stripy paper straw? What else in your kitchen could you use, if you don't have the recommended glass – a hollowed-out Easter egg? A pineapple-shaped mug that was previously just a happy holiday souvenir?

A blender is essential for many cocktails, to really mingle the Baileys with the other ingredients, but for lighter cocktails a shaker is all you'll need, so don't sweat it! For a perfect party, you may find it's worth getting a cocktail shaker kit, which usually includes the shaker plus strainer, muddler, long spoon and measuring jigger, so you can really feel the part as you mix and measure like a pro. You'll often be filling the shaker with the ingredients plus some ice, so, once shaken and strained through the perforated cap or strainer, you'll have a delicious, cool cocktail in your glass, ready to toast.

The milk frother is ideal for the creaminess of some of the Baileys cocktails, and gives the wonderful bubbles on top of simple recipes like the sublimely rich Sublime Chococcino (see page 25). Treat yourself, indeed!

Year-round, you'll find the perfect Baileys cocktail for you, whether it's a refreshing Strawberry Daiquiri (see page 68) in the heat of the summer when all you can do is lie on a deckchair, or the perfect indulgence of an extravagant Nutterlicious Cocktail (see page 128) when you're snuggled beneath the fairy lights. Cheers!

EQUIPMENT
Blender
Cocktail shaker
Milk frother
Tall glasses
Martini glasses
Balloon glasses
Shot glasses
Tumblers

BAKING EQUIPMENT

Baking is always about indulgence. While some baking can be more scientific, Baileys baking is about enjoyment in the moment, the pleasure of sharing with friends, the spontaneity of whipping up something scrumptious and fun to enjoy right now.

The 'essential' equipment here will make life a lot easier for you when you want to dig into one of the delicious Baileys treats (a clean tea towel over the shoulder is vital while cooking anything, surely, and an electric hand whisk serves to mix, aerate, smooth and much more), but for the 'useful' list, you can be more flexible.

Don't worry if you don't have the exact 'right' thing; Baileys desserts will be sublime in any measure. No piping bag? Try a plastic bag with the corner chopped off. Missing baking beans from your cupboard? Uncooked rice on your baking parchment will do much the same job. Experiment with the equipment you do have – an electric whisk, a good knife and a chopping board, and non-stick baking parchment and baking sheets can go a long way. Check your recipe for any particular equipment like lolly sticks or chocolate moulds that may be a one-off, and for the specific dimensions of the cake tins or baking dishes, but it's still worth making even if they don't match what's in your cupboard. Whatever you do – enjoy your finished treat. It'll be out-of-this-world delicious!

ESSENTIAL

Electric hand whisk
Balloon whisk
Non-stick baking parchment
Rolling pin
Clean tea towel
3 baking sheets
40cm x 30cm Swiss roll tin
12-hole muffin tin
Ovenproof baking dish
Sharp knife and chopping board
Saucepan

USEFUL

Mini food processor
Digital thermometer
Milk frother
Blender
Blowtorch
Small (20cm) frying pan
Large (30cm) frying pan
900g loaf tin
Cake tins: springform, flan tins, square tins and sandwich tins
Paper muffin cases and mini cases
Small palette knife
Baking beans
Piping bags and plain nozzles
Shallow, lidded plastic container
Serving dishes: ramekins, small glasses, glass bowls, teacups, sundae glasses and mugs
Fluted and plain pastry cutters

Baileys

SPRING

~~~~~~

Is that ... sunlight out there? The days are finally getting longer, and we're dusting off our sunglasses to get out and share these scrummy springtime pick-me-ups. It's a good time to have a good time, and a box of fluffy Divine Doughnuts (see page 20), dreamy little clouds of joy, is certainly going to make these moments even more delicious, whether on a park bench or drying off at your best friend's place. For your first brunch of the new season, how about a heaped, mouth-watering plate of Delectable French Toast with Raspberries (see page 18), with maybe a warming Sublime Chococcino (see page 25) to follow? And on 17 March, who could possibly refuse a gloriously decadent and oh-so-green sprinkle-topped St Patrick's Day Milkshake (see page 30) ...?

~~~~~~

Chocolatini
CUPCAKES

Who said you need a special occasion to indulge in these luxurious cupcakes? A birthday, a good day at work, a really average day at work, or a picnic in the park. Sounds like it's time for Chocolatini Cupcakes.

EQUIPMENT

12-hole muffin tin
12 paper muffin cases
electric hand whisk
small palette knife

INGREDIENTS

175g butter, softened
175g light brown sugar
2 large eggs, beaten
50g cocoa powder
100ml Baileys
150g plain flour
½ tsp bicarbonate
   of soda
1 tsp baking powder

FOR THE BUTTERCREAM

60g butter, softened
60g full-fat cream
   cheese
180g icing sugar
2 tbsp Baileys
1 tsp cocoa powder,
   to decorate
chocolate sprinkles, to
   decorate (optional)

1. Preheat the oven to 180°C/fan 160°C/gas 4. Line the muffin tin with paper cases.

2. In a large bowl beat the butter and the sugar with a whisk until they are light and fluffy. Add the egg, a little at a time, beating well between each addition.

3. Add the cocoa powder and the Baileys alternately, a little at a time, and beat until they are smooth. Sift in the flour, bicarbonate of soda and baking powder and fold them in gently until everything is fully combined.

4. Spoon the mixture into the muffin cases and bake the cupcakes in the oven for 15–20 minutes until they are risen and a skewer inserted in the middle of one comes out clean. Cool them for 5 minutes in the tin, then remove them to a wire rack and leave them to cool completely.

5. Meanwhile make the buttercream. Beat the butter and cream cheese together and gradually add the icing sugar, beating well between each addition, until the mixture is thick and creamy. Finally, add the Baileys and beat again.

6. Once the cakes are completely cool, top each with buttercream and swirl with a small palette knife. Sift with cocoa powder and finish with a few chocolate sprinkles, then it's time to share your delicious chocolatey efforts.

Delectable
FRENCH TOAST
WITH RASPBERRIES

Try This

Fry streaky bacon slices until crisp and serve them with the French toast and a drizzle of maple syrup for the full American diner breakfast experience.

Do you know what's a real vibe? French toast with creamy Baileys and fresh raspberries. Don't bother saving it for the perfect weekend; cook it now and create your own perfect weekend.

You can thank us later.

EQUIPMENT

large frying pan

INGREDIENTS

2 large eggs
50ml milk
50ml Baileys
4 thick slices of brioche
10g butter
2 tbsp sunflower oil
200g raspberries
Icing sugar, to dust

1 In a large bowl lightly beat the eggs with a fork, add the milk and Baileys and beat again to combine.

2 Dip a slice of brioche into the egg mix, leave it to soak for a few seconds, then turn it over and soak it again. Place the slice on a plate and repeat with the remaining slices.

3 Heat the butter and a tablespoon of the sunflower oil in the frying pan until the butter has melted and is starting to foam. Put two slices of the brioche in the pan and fry them for 2 minutes until they are golden, then turn them over and cook the other side. Remove them to a plate to keep warm. Add the remaining tablespoon of oil to the pan and repeat with the other two slices of brioche.

4 Scatter over some raspberries, dust with icing sugar and serve immediately, enjoying every mouthful of the perfect casual indulgence.

Divine
DOUGHNUTS

Did someone say fresh, sugary doughnuts? Filled with a creamy Baileys custard? Whether it's a stunning spring afternoon or a drizzly evening, who could say no to these dreamy little clouds of joy?

electric hand whisk

balloon whisk

rolling pin

5cm or 6cm plain
   pastry cutter

3 baking trays

digital thermometer

slotted spoon

piping bag with plain
   1cm nozzle

1) Melt the butter in a small pan over a low heat, add the milk and gently heat for another minute until it is lukewarm. Remove the pan from the heat and beat in the eggs and sugar.

2) Tip the flour into a large bowl, or the bowl of a freestanding mixer fitted with a dough hook. Stir in the salt, then sprinkle over the yeast, create a well in the centre and pour in the milk and egg mix. Then, if using a mixer, mix on a low setting to combine before increasing the speed to medium and kneading for 5–10 minutes until the dough is smooth and elastic. If making by hand, stir the flour into the milk with a spoon to create a rough dough, then tip it on to the work surface and bring it together with your hands. The mixture will be sticky at first but once you start kneading it will firm up, so resist the temptation to add much extra flour. Knead for 10 minutes until you have a smooth and elastic dough.

INGREDIENTS

50g butter

250ml full-fat milk

2 medium eggs

50g caster sugar

500g strong white
bread flour

1 tsp salt

7g packet fast-action
dried yeast

sunflower oil, for
deep frying

FOR THE CUSTARD FILLING

100ml Baileys

150ml full-fat milk

3 medium egg yolks

60g caster sugar

40g plain flour

1 tsp vanilla bean paste

100ml double cream

FOR THE SUGAR COATING

75g caster sugar

1 tsp ground cinnamon

3. Lightly oil a clean mixing bowl, put the dough in it and cover it with cling film. Leave the bowl in a warm place for 1–1½ hours until the dough has doubled in size.

4. Meanwhile make the custard filling. Heat the Baileys and milk in a medium pan until they start to bubble at the edges. Whisk the egg yolks, sugar and flour in a mixing bowl until they are combined. Pour the hot Baileys mixture on to the paste, whisking as you pour. Add the vanilla bean paste, then pour the custard back into the pan. Heat over a low heat for 5–10 minutes, whisking constantly with a balloon whisk until the filling is very thick and creamy. Pour the thickened custard into a bowl, cover the surface with cling film to stop a skin forming, then leave it to cool before putting the bowl in the fridge to cool completely.

5. Whisk the double cream until soft peaks form and fold it into the cooled custard, then return it to the fridge while you finish the doughnuts.

6. Once the dough has risen, tip it on to a lightly floured work surface and knead it once or twice to knock out any excess air. Using a rolling pin, roll out the dough until it is 2.5cm thick. Dust the pastry cutter with flour and cut out 12 rounds from the dough. Place the rounds on a baking tray lined with baking parchment and leave them to prove for about 30 minutes until they have doubled in size.

7. During the last 5–10 minutes of proving time, pour the oil into a large, deep-sided pan and heat it until it reaches 160°C. Lay sheets of kitchen paper on the second baking tray and mix the caster sugar and cinnamon on the third to coat the doughnuts.

8 Using a slotted spoon, gently lower the doughnuts into the hot oil four at a time. Fry them for 4 minutes, turning them over after 2 minutes, until they are golden on both sides. Remove them from the pan and drain them on the kitchen paper before tossing them in the cinnamon sugar while still warm. Deep fry the remaining doughnuts in two more batches.

9 Leave the doughnuts to cool, then use the end of a teaspoon to make a hole in the side of each one. Fit the piping nozzle into the end of the piping bag and fill the bag with the cooled custard. Push the nozzle into the hole in each doughnut and pipe in the custard. Best eaten on the day you make them, shared with friends, and enjoyed with very sugary lips.

Try This

Don't want to fry? Divide the dough into 12 pieces, roll each piece into a ball and leave them to prove as above. Butter the holes of a 12-hole muffin tin with a little melted butter, brush each risen ball with more butter and place them in the holes of the muffin tin. Bake at 200°C/fan 180°C/gas 6 for 15 minutes until golden. Cool the doughnuts on a wire rack, then split them through the middle and fill with the custard.

Swirled
BROWNIES

The only thing better than a brownie is a Baileys brownie, with creamy white chocolate and smooth peanut butter, swirled into perfection.

EQUIPMENT

30 x 20cm baking tin

non-stick baking parchment

electric hand whisk

INGREDIENTS

FOR THE SWIRL

100ml Baileys

100g white chocolate

2 tbsp smooth peanut butter

FOR THE BROWNIES

200g butter

300g dark chocolate, broken into chunks

300g light brown sugar

4 large eggs

225g plain flour

100g pecans, roughly chopped

1 Preheat the oven to 180°C/fan 160°C/gas 4. Grease and line the baking tin with baking parchment.

2 For the swirl, heat the Baileys in a small pan until it starts to bubble at the edges, remove from the heat, add the white chocolate and stir until melted. Add the peanut butter, beat until smooth and set aside while you make the brownie mix.

3 Put the butter and chocolate in a heatproof bowl and either melt them in the microwave or set the bowl over a pan of gently simmering water. Stir to combine and when all the chocolate chunks have melted, remove the bowl and set it aside.

4 In a large bowl whisk the sugar and eggs until they are pale and thick, add the chocolate and butter mix and whisk again. Tip in the flour and pecans and fold them in until they are fully incorporated. Pour the mixture into the baking tin.

5 Dollop teaspoons of the swirl mix on top of the brownie mix at regular intervals, then swirl it in using the tip of a skewer or the end of a teaspoon. Bake the brownie in the oven for 25–30 minutes until the top is firm to the touch and the surface is starting to crack. Leave it to cool for 10 minutes in the tin, then transfer it to a wire rack and allow it to cool completely.

6 Cut into 20 squares and store in an airtight container for up to five days (not that they will stick around that long, anyway).

Sublime
CHOCOCCINO

A super-simple, warming treat for spring evenings when you need a little spontaneous indulgence. Your go-to mug, your favourite chocolate and a dash of Baileys.

What more could you want?

EQUIPMENT

milk frother

INGREDIENTS

25g milk chocolate, finely grated, plus a little extra for topping

1 tbsp Baileys

200ml milk

1 Mix the chocolate and Baileys in a mug and stir well to combine.

2 Heat the milk in a small pan or milk frothing jug until it just starts to simmer. Remove the pan from the heat and froth the milk with the top of the jug or an electric milk frother.

3 Pour the milk into the mug, stirring as you pour, and top with a final layer of frothy milk. Add a little extra grated chocolate to the top, snuggle up and savour the treat you've deserved all day.

Try This

If you don't have a milk frother put half the hot milk in a jam jar, secure the lid and wrap the jar in a tea towel – this helps to keep the milk warm and also protects you against any leaks of hot milk! Shake the jar vigorously until the milk is frothy and mix it with the hot chocolate as above.

Tasty
TINY TARTS

An easy, mini springtime treat for weekday get-togethers or weekend gatherings, these little tarts look iconic, taste divine and will impress every crowd at any-sized table.

EQUIPMENT

baking sheet

INGREDIENTS

18 shortcrust pastry tartlet cases

100ml Baileys

1 tbsp light brown sugar

150g dark chocolate, broken into chunks

18 mini chocolate eggs or raspberries

1) Arrange the pastry cases on a baking sheet, brushing out any loose crumbs. Heat the Baileys and sugar in a pan over a gentle heat until the sugar has melted and the Baileys has started to bubble. Remove the pan from the heat, add the chocolate chunks and beat the mixture until it is smooth.

2) Spoon a teaspoonful of chocolate into each pastry case then leave the tartlets to cool for 5–10 minutes before topping each with a mini chocolate egg or raspberry. Leave the tartlets to set completely. Plate up for some of the prettiest treats in town.

Try This

Whip 75ml of double cream until soft peaks form, whisk in 1 tablespoon of Baileys then swirl a teaspoonful of the mixture on top of each tart.

Birthday Cake
PARTY SHOT

You know what they say, it's somebody's birthday somewhere. Right? We haven't all got time to bake a whole cake, so why not try this party in a glass? It's easy, yummy and ideal for a celebration wherever you are.

EQUIPMENT

cocktail shaker

shot glass

INGREDIENTS

25ml Baileys

1 tbsp Smirnoff Iced Cake Vodka or vanilla vodka

handful of ice

FOR TOPPING

whipped cream

multicoloured sprinkles

1) Pour the Baileys and the vodka into a cocktail shaker with a handful of ice and shake it well to combine.

2) Strain the mixture into a shot glass and top with the whipped cream and sprinkles. There you go — birthday cake in a glass!

Luxurious
TRUFFLES

Make something sweet for the one you love this spring – and by this we mean yourself. Embrace a moment with these creamy, decadent truffles with hidden raspberry delight.

EQUIPMENT

mini food processor

baking sheet

non-stick baking parchment

20 mini paper cases

INGREDIENTS

150ml double cream

150g milk chocolate, broken into small chunks

100g dark chocolate (70% cocoa solids), broken into small chunks

3 tbsp Baileys

1 tbsp cocoa powder

9g freeze-dried raspberry pieces

1. Heat the cream in a medium pan until it just starts to boil. Remove the pan from the heat, tip in the milk and dark chocolate and stir well until they have melted. Stir in the Baileys a tablespoon at a time, beating well between each addition to form a smooth ganache.

2. Transfer the mixture to a bowl, cover and chill it for 2 hours until it is firm.

3. Sift the cocoa powder into a small bowl. Blitz the raspberry pieces in a mini food processor for a few minutes to create tiny fragments and tip these into another small bowl.

4. Use a teaspoon to scoop out 20 pieces of the chilled ganache and place them on a baking sheet lined with baking parchment. If the ganache is still a bit sticky, pop the baking sheet in the fridge for about 10 minutes. Roll each truffle into a ball, coat half of them in cocoa powder and half in the raspberry dust, then pop each coated truffle into a paper case and chill them in the fridge. Box them up for a gift, or keep them chilled and ready for a mouthful of pleasure if you need a little moment.

St Patrick's Day
MILKSHAKE

Happy St Patrick's Day!

Today is the perfect excuse to get a little extra with your drinks. To start you off, we'd highly recommend whipping up this decadent green milkshake.

EQUIPMENT

blender

sundae glass

INGREDIENTS

50ml Baileys

100ml milk

2 scoops mint choc chip ice-cream

chocolate sauce, to swirl

FOR TOPPING

50ml double cream or whipped or squirty cream

1 tsp chopped mixed nuts or pistachios

1 tbsp mini meringues

1 tsp green sprinkles

1 Pour the Baileys and milk into a blender and add the ice-cream. Blend them until they reach a consistency you like. Add more ice-cream if you want.

2 Swirl some chocolate sauce around the inside of the sundae glass.

3 Pour the mixture into the sundae glass and top it with whipped cream, chopped nuts, mini meringues, green sprinkles – anything green and tasty you can find.

4 Raise your glasses to St Patrick – sláinte!

Cool Berry
COCONUT SMOOTHIE

SERVES
2

PREP TIME
15
MINS

When the weather starts warming up and the days get longer, it's 100 per cent the most delicious time to taste the fresh flavours of spring. Share this delish recipe with a friend, even if the weather isn't (yet) as tropical as the smoothie.

EQUIPMENT

blender
tall glasses

INGREDIENTS

135ml Baileys
150g Greek yoghurt
150g frozen blueberries
250ml coconut milk
1 banana, sliced

FOR TOPPING
handful of berries
coconut flakes

1. To make the bottom layer, blend 45ml of the Baileys with 75g of the yoghurt and 100g of the blueberries until the mixture is smooth.

2. Divide the mixture between two tall glasses.

3. To make the middle layer, blend 45ml of the Baileys with the remaining 75g of yoghurt, the rest of the blueberries and 125ml of the coconut milk until the mixture is smooth.

4. Carefully spoon the mixture into the glasses on top of the base layer. Rinse out the blender.

5. To make the top layer, blend the last 45ml of the Baileys with the banana and the remaining 125ml of coconut milk.

6. Spoon the mixture into the glasses on top of the middle layer. Add a few berries and coconut flakes to decorate and serve immediately, imagining you're on a beautiful beach in the spring sunshine.

Glorious
ZABAGLIONE

**SERVES
4**

PREP TIME
**20
MINS**

One of the most incredible
delights of travelling is
discovering new foods, but when
you can't go to Italy, why not
bring those Italian flavours to
you with this indulgent treat?

EQUIPMENT

electric hand whisk

4 small glasses

INGREDIENTS

4 large egg yolks

4 tbsp golden
caster sugar

4 tbsp Baileys

grated nutmeg, to serve

1) Half-fill a pan with water then set it over a medium heat
and bring the water to a gentle simmer.

2) Find a large mixing bowl that fits on top of the pan without
the base touching the water. Remove the bowl and put
the egg yolks and sugar in it. Whisk the eggs and sugar
until they are thick and creamy, then add the Baileys a
tablespoon at a time, whisking between each addition.

3) Once you've added all the Baileys set the bowl on top of
the pan. Continue whisking until the mixture is very thick
and creamy and the whisk leaves a ribbon trail that holds its
shape for a few seconds when you lift it out. This will take
10–15 minutes of whisking.

4) Remove the bowl from the heat and divide the zabaglione
between the glasses. Top each with a little grated nutmeg
and serve immediately. A wonderful little glass of Italy.

Dreamy
MINI CHEESECAKES

Small but perfectly formed –
and even if they're imperfectly
formed, they're still scrumptious.
Plus you can go for seconds, and
thirds (see photo overleaf).

(see photo overleaf)

EQUIPMENT

4 x 8cm metal
dessert rings

baking sheet

non-stick baking
parchment

balloon whisk

1. Grease the insides of the dessert rings with a little of the melted butter and place them on the baking sheet lined with a piece of baking parchment.

2. Pop the biscuits into a plastic food bag and crush them with a rolling pin to create crumbs. Tip the crumbs into a bowl with the melted butter and stir to combine everything. Divide the crumb mixture between the dessert rings and press it down inside each one to create a smooth base – use the base of a small bottle or jar to create an even layer. Chill the bases in the fridge while you make the filling.

3. Put the gelatine leaves in a bowl of cold water and leave them to soften for 5 minutes. Meanwhile heat the Baileys in a small pan until it just starts to simmer. Remove the pan from the heat and squeeze any excess water from each gelatine leaf before adding it to the pan. Stir until the leaves have melted.

INGREDIENTS

50g butter, melted

100g Biscoff biscuits

2 gelatine leaves

100ml Baileys

180g full-fat
   cream cheese

100g Greek yoghurt

100g icing sugar

1 tsp vanilla bean paste

handful of crushed
   mini eggs or berries
   such as redcurrants,
   to decorate

4. Put the cream cheese, yoghurt, sugar and vanilla bean paste into a medium bowl and beat them with a balloon whisk until they are smooth. Pour the Baileys mixture into the bowl and whisk again.

5. Divide the filling between the chilled bases, smoothing the tops once all four are filled. Gently tap the baking sheet on the work surface to give them a smooth top. Chill the cheesecakes for at least 2 hours until they are set.

6. To serve, run a small, round-bladed knife around the inside of each dessert ring before lifting it off. Place the cheesecakes on a plate and decorate them with a scattering of redcurrants. Taste the dreamy, creamy cheesecakes with that perfect Baileys lift.

Try This!

You could also serve this with a raspberry coulis. In a small pan gently heat 200g raspberries until they start to soften. Remove the pan from the heat and pass the raspberries through a sieve. Stir in 50g of icing sugar and leave the coulis to cool. Drizzle it over the cheesecakes in place of the redcurrants.

Pure Pleasure
CUSTARD TART

An absolute classic, this custard tart has a delicious chocolate pastry case to bring out the rich Baileys flavour of the custard filling. Serve as a dessert round the table, or pack it up for a dreamy picnic outdoors (see photo on previous page).

EQUIPMENT

rolling pin

23cm fluted, loose-
   bottomed flan tin

baking sheet

non-stick baking
   parchment

baking beans

electric hand whisk

1. Put the flour and cocoa powder into a large mixing bowl and add the butter cubes. Rub the butter into the flour with your fingertips until the mixture resembles breadcrumbs. Stir in the sugar, then add the egg and 2 tablespoons of cold water and bring everything together to form a soft dough – add a dash more water if needed. Wrap the dough in cling film and leave it to chill in the fridge for 30 minutes.

2. On a lightly-floured surface roll the pastry into a circle the thickness of a £1 coin and large enough to line the flan tin. Carefully lift the pastry on the rolling pin and lay it over the tin. Ease the pastry into the base of the tin and up the sides and use a small ball of pastry to gently push the base into the edges of the tin and the flutes around the sides. Roll the rolling pin over the top of the flan tin to remove any

INGREDIENTS

230g plain flour, plus extra for dusting

30g cocoa powder

150g butter, chilled and cut into cubes

60g caster sugar

1 large egg, lightly beaten

flowers, to decorate (optional)

FOR THE CUSTARD FILLING

6 large egg yolks

75g caster sugar

500ml double cream

100ml Baileys

excess pastry. Prick the base with a fork and chill it in the fridge for 30 minutes. This second chilling stops the pastry shrinking as it cooks.

3 Preheat the oven to 200°C/fan 180°C/gas 6. Place the flan tin on a baking sheet, scrunch up a sheet of baking parchment and place it inside the pastry, then fill it with baking beans. Bake the base in the oven for 15 minutes, then remove the baking parchment and beans and bake for a further 5 minutes until the base is cooked.

4 Meanwhile make the custard filling. In a large bowl whisk the egg yolks and sugar until they are pale and thick. Heat the cream and Baileys until they just start to simmer, then pour them over the egg yolk mix, whisking as you pour, until everything is fully incorporated. Pour the mixture into a large jug and set it aside.

5 Once the pastry case is cooked, turn down the oven to 150°C/fan 130°C/gas 2, pull out the oven shelf with the baking tin still on it and slowly pour in the custard. Slide the shelf back into the oven and bake the tart for 35–40 minutes until the custard starts to turn golden but still has a slight wobble in the middle.

6 Remove the tart from the oven, place it on a wire rack and leave it to cool completely.

7 Remove the tart from the tin and place it on a serving plate. Serve it immediately or chill it for a few hours before serving it in slices with a dollop of crème fraîche or a drizzle of cream, a feel-good pleasure for any spring gathering.

Flat White
MARTINI

Martini, anyone? Smooth and creamy, this coffee cocktail is just right for those evenings in the garden with friends or kitchen catch-ups.

EQUIPMENT

cocktail shaker
martini glass

INGREDIENTS

50ml Baileys
15ml (1 tbsp) vodka
25ml espresso
handful of ice
3 coffee beans,
 to decorate

1) Pour the liquid ingredients into a cocktail shaker, add the ice, seal the shaker and shake it vigorously until everything is blended and the liquid is as smooth as silk.

2) Strain the mixture into a martini glass and garnish it with the three coffee beans. Serve immediately. It's cocktail time – cheers!

Rocky
ROAD

CHILLING TIME
2
HOURS

MAKES
25

PREP TIME
15
MINS

Sweet, crunchy, squidgy, chocolatey – and all with a hint of heavenly Baileys. This rocky road is a scrumptious treat for all chocolate-lovers, made for those 'dessert for dinner' moments or when you just feel like treating yourself.

EQUIPMENT

20cm square shallow cake tin

non-stick baking parchment

INGREDIENTS

100g butter, plus extra for greasing

150g dark chocolate, broken into chunks

150g milk chocolate, broken into chunks

60ml Baileys

150g digestive biscuits

75g mini marshmallows

50g pistachios, roughly chopped

50g raisins

1. Grease and line the cake tin with baking parchment.

2. Put the dark and milk chocolate into a large heatproof bowl with the butter and Baileys and melt them over a pan of gently simmering water, or on a medium heat in a microwave. Stir until the chocolate and butter have melted and you have a thick glossy mixture.

3. Break the biscuits into pieces – some larger than others – and add them to the bowl along with the marshmallows, pistachios and raisins. Stir to coat everything in chocolate, then spoon the mixture into the prepared cake tin and spread it out in an even layer.

4. Place the cake tin in the fridge for 2 hours to set, then remove the rocky road from the tin and cut it into 25 squares. Store in an airtight container in the fridge for up to a week, or share it with friends for an al fresco spring treat.

Meringue
NESTS

COOKING TIME
1 HOUR

SERVES
6

PREP TIME
25 MINS

Nothing says spring like meringue nests, filled with rich Baileys cream and early-summer fruits. Pile them high and let the drips and splashes create a luxurious platter of pudding pleasure.

You'll never look back.

EQUIPMENT

2 baking sheets

non-stick baking parchment

electric hand whisk

INGREDIENTS

3 large egg whites

180g caster sugar

1 tsp cornflour

1 tsp white wine vinegar

300ml double cream

75ml Baileys

300g frozen summer fruits, defrosted

Try This

Replace the summer fruits with cubes of fresh mango and a spoonful of passion fruit flesh or a drizzle of passion fruit and mango coulis.

1. Line the baking sheets with baking parchment. Preheat the oven to 120°C/fan 100°C/gas 1.

2. Put the egg whites into a large bowl and whisk them until stiff peaks form. Add the sugar a spoonful at a time, whisking well between each addition. Add the cornflour and white wine vinegar with the last of the sugar.

3. Place a large spoonful of meringue on a baking sheet and shape it into a round, making a slight indent in the middle. Repeat with the rest of the meringue to create six nests in total.

4. Bake the meringues in the oven for 1 hour until they are firm and crisp. Turn off the oven, prop open the oven door a crack and leave the meringues to cool. Remove the baking sheet from the oven and leave the meringues to cool completely before removing them from the baking parchment.

5. Whisk the cream until soft peaks form, add the Baileys and whisk again. Divide the cream between the meringue nests, top with a spoonful of the summer fruit and serve them immediately (or the meringues can be made in advance and stored in an airtight container for up to a week). Enjoy the bright colours of the nests and the creamy, fresh flavours as you dig in.

Baileys
SUMMER

Time to break out the picnic blanket! It's the season for al-fresco meet-ups, garden hang-outs and campfire get-togethers, the perfect opportunity for some cool drinks and some even cooler desserts. What better excuse to grab an extra spoon and dig into a cool and creamy Summery Sundae (see page 58), or a daydreamy Delicious Dublin Mess (see page 48), our own version of the classic with a Baileys twist? How about some fluffy Whoopie Pies (see page 54) for an extra-special picnic treat – and when you're sitting in the sun, we're 100 per cent sure there's nothing better than enjoying a cream-spice-ready-for-ice Spiced Cold Brew (see page 67) in a deckchair with friends.

Delicious
DUBLIN MESS

A gorgeous Irish version of this sumptuous summer dessert, in honour of the iconic Irish cream and whiskey that goes into every bottle. An ideal treat for daydreaming in the sunshine.

EQUIPMENT

electric hand whisk
6 glass bowls

INGREDIENTS

4 meringue nests
200g strawberries
600ml double cream
100ml Baileys,
    plus a little extra
    for drizzling

1. Break the meringue nests into small pieces and hull and quarter the strawberries. Reserve 12 strawberry quarters and a few pieces of meringue for decoration.

2. Lightly whisk the cream until soft peaks form and add the Baileys, 50ml at a time, whisking between each addition.

3. Gently fold in the strawberry pieces and then the meringue pieces. Divide the mixture between the bowls and top with the reserved strawberry quarters and meringue pieces.

4. Finish with a final drizzle of Baileys over the bright, fresh strawberries, and share immediately with your friends for a stunning and simple sweet.

Salted Caramel
FUDGE

A yummy treat for the warmer months, fudge reminds us of summer holidays and beach trips, huge chunks of it in striped paper bags. This only takes a little time to make, but gives you enough for yourself, and leftovers for a gift. *What more could you want?*

EQUIPMENT

20cm square tin

non-stick baking
 parchment

digital thermometer

electric hand whisk

INGREDIENTS

120g butter, plus
 extra for greasing

397g tin caramel
 condensed milk

100ml full-fat milk

50ml Baileys

400g light brown sugar

1 tsp sea salt

1) Grease and line the tin with baking parchment.

2) Put all the ingredients except the salt into a large pan and heat them over a gentle heat until the sugar has dissolved, the butter has melted and you have a thick glossy sauce. Increase the heat until the mixture is bubbling and cook until the temperature reaches 116°C on a thermometer, stirring occasionally to prevent the fudge catching. This will take 10–15 minutes.

3) Once the mixture reaches the right temperature remove the pan from the heat and leave the fudge for 5 minutes to cool slightly, then beat in the sea salt. Beat with the whisk for 5–10 minutes until the fudge thickens and has lost its gloss – this makes it smooth and creamy.

4) Pour the fudge into the prepared tin and leave it to cool and set for a few hours.

5) Remove the fudge from the tin and cut it into 36 squares. It will keep for up to two weeks stored in an airtight container, or take it along in some paper bags to your next catch-up with friends and share the deliciousness.

Sensational
CHOCOLATE ROULADE

This is a showstopper of a summer dessert. A swirly, sumptuous treat that's a perfect end to any meal, or just for when you're feeling your best self – because those spontaneous, in-the-moment delights are the best ones, don't you agree?

EQUIPMENT

40 x 30cm Swiss roll tin

non-stick baking parchment

electric hand whisk

clean tea towel

1 Preheat the oven to 200°C/180°C fan/gas 6. Grease and line the Swiss roll tin with baking parchment.

2 In a large mixing bowl whisk together the eggs and caster sugar for about 5 minutes until you have a very thick and pale mixture. Lift the whisk out of the mixture and move it across the bowl to check that the trail it leaves keeps its shape for a few seconds.

3 Sift the cocoa powder over the cake batter and gently fold it in until it is fully incorporated. Pour the batter into the tin, carefully level the surface and bake it for 10–12 minutes until it is just firm to the touch.

COOKING TIME
10–12
MINS

SERVES
8–10

PREP TIME
20
MINS

INGREDIENTS

butter, for greasing

4 large eggs

120g caster sugar, plus extra for sprinkling

60g cocoa powder

FOR THE FILLING

50g mascarpone cheese

50ml Baileys

100ml double cream

150g raspberries, halved lengthways

4) While the roulade is baking, lay a sheet of baking parchment on a wire cooling rack and sprinkle an even layer of caster sugar over it. Remove the cake from the oven and turn it out of the tin on to the sugar-coated parchment. Carefully peel the parchment from the bottom of the roulade, cover it with a clean tea towel and leave it to cool.

5) For the filling, beat the mascarpone to soften it, add the Baileys and beat again. In another bowl whisk the cream until soft peaks form, then whisk in the Baileys and mascarpone mixture.

6) Unroll the roulade, it may crack a little but don't worry the frosting will cover the cracks. Spread a third of the frosting onto the sponge, then re-roll and place on a serving plate, seam side down. Cut a quarter off the end of the cake at an angle and attach to the side of the cake with a little frosting. Spread the remaining icing all over the yule log, including the ends, and with a fork swirl in a pattern to resemble bark. Dust with a little icing sugar and add a robin or two and some trees on the side of the plate to create a Christmassy scene.

7) Alternatively leave the roulade whole and smooth the icing to an even layer scatter over white chocolate stars and leave to set before cutting into slices to serve.

Whoopie PIES

Sweet and fluffy, these whoopie pies are literally the most incredible little treats, if we do say so ourselves. Like mini chocolate-and-marshmallow sandwiches, they're the irresistible grown-up choice for a picnic in the park or BBQ when the weather's on your side.

EQUIPMENT

2 baking sheets

non-stick baking parchment

electric hand whisk

INGREDIENTS

120g butter, softened

200g light brown sugar

1 large egg

240g plain flour

60g cocoa powder

1 tsp bicarbonate of soda

300ml buttermilk

FOR THE FILLING

120g butter, softened

200g icing sugar

213g jar marshmallow fluff

2 tbsp Baileys

1 Preheat the oven to 180°C/fan 160°C/gas 4. Line each baking sheet with baking parchment.

2 Put the pie ingredients into a large mixing bowl and beat them together with the whisk until you have a thick and creamy mixture.

3 Use a tablespoon to scoop blobs of the mixture on to the baking sheets. Aim for 12 per sheet and leave a 2–3cm gap between between them to allow them to spread as they bake.

4 Bake the pies in the oven for 12–14 minutes until they are a dark chocolate brown and firm to the touch. Leave them on the baking sheets for a couple of minutes before moving them to wire racks with a palette knife to cool completely.

5 Meanwhile make the filling. Put the butter, icing sugar, marshmallow fluff and Baileys into a large bowl and beat them together with the whisk. Beat on a slow speed to start with until the icing sugar is all mixed in to keep the sugar cloud to a minimum. Then beat for 2–3 minutes more until the mixture is thick and creamy.

6 Spread a spoonful of the marshmallow filling on the flat side of one of the pie halves and top it with another half. Repeat with the remaining pies, until you have assembled all 12 of them. They will keep for three or four days in an airtight container, but it's unlikely they'll remain uneaten in that time. Share with friends at your next al fresco get-together.

Delicious
ICED COFFEE

The only reason you need to make this indulgent and delicious iced coffee is that it tastes unreal on a warm day. And two scoops of ice-cream? *Well, why the hell not?*

EQUIPMENT

blender

electric hand whisk

2 tall glasses

INGREDIENTS

100ml Baileys

2 large scoops vanilla ice-cream

200ml full-fat milk

150ml double cream

a handful of ice

300ml freshly brewed and cooled coffee

2 tbsp chocolate sauce

1 tbsp chopped toasted hazelnuts

1 Whizz the Baileys in a blender with the ice-cream and milk. Whip the cream in a bowl until soft peaks form.

2 Half-fill the glasses with ice. Pour over the Baileys mixture followed by the cooled coffee.

3 Spoon whipped cream on top, generously drizzle over the chocolate sauce, then sprinkle the top with chopped nuts to give you the perfect coffee cool-down. Relax, and enjoy.

Summery SUNDAES

SERVES
2

PREP TIME
10
MINS

Every day is a sundae day when it's summer, right? A tall glass, cool ice-cream, rich brownies and delightful Baileys. That's what we like to call levelling up your treats with the sweetest of goodness.

EQUIPMENT

balloon whisk

2 sundae glasses

INGREDIENTS

2 tbsp dark
  chocolate sauce

4 tbsp Baileys

100ml double cream

4 tbsp summer
  fruit compote

2 brownies, broken
  in half

4 scoops vanilla
  ice-cream

2 small chocolate
  flakes, to decorate

1 Gently heat the chocolate sauce, either in a heatproof bowl in a microwave or in a small pan over a low heat, until it is just warmed through. Remove from the heat, stir in 2 tablespoons of the Baileys and set the sauce aside to cool.

2 Whisk the cream until soft peaks form, then add the remaining 2 tablespoons of Baileys and whisk again.

3 Put 1 tablespoon of fruit compote in the bottom of each sundae glass and top it with a piece of brownie and a scoop of ice-cream. Drizzle a little of the Baileys chocolate sauce over each ice-cream scoop, then repeat the layers, saving a little of the chocolate sauce for the top.

4 Top the sundaes with whipped cream – spoon or pipe it on in a swirl – and drizzle over the last of the chocolate sauce. Decorate each sundae with a flake, admire it for just a moment, then tuck in.

Choco MOUSSE

CHILLING TIME
3 HOURS

SERVES
6

PREP TIME
30 MINS

With layers of total deliciousness, these choco mousses are easy on the eye and even better in the mouth. When the sun's gone down on a late-night feast, serve with sparklers if you feel like being a little bit extra.

EQUIPMENT

electric hand whisk
6 small glasses

INGREDIENTS

150g dark chocolate, broken into pieces
1 tsp unsalted butter
2 medium eggs, separated
200ml Baileys
300ml double cream
chocolate shavings, to decorate

1. Put the chocolate and butter in a heatproof bowl over a pan of gently simmering water and heat them until they melt, or melt them in a microwave on a medium heat. Allow the mixture to cool slightly, then beat in the egg yolks and add 100ml of the Baileys a little at a time, beating well between each addition.

2. Lightly whip the cream until soft peaks form and add the remaining 100ml of Baileys to it. Whisk again and then fold half the cream into the chocolate mix.

3. Whisk the egg whites until they are just stiff. Stir a spoonful into the chocolate mix to loosen it and then fold in the rest until everything is combined.

4. Spoon half the chocolate mousse into six small glasses and top them with half the cream. Repeat the layers and sprinkle chocolate shavings over the top of each glass.

5. Put the glasses in the fridge for 3 hours. No picking (well, maybe just a bit ...). Serve with a flourish to some impressed oohs and aahs.

Strawberry
SWISS ROLL

With a fluffy sponge, creamy Baileys filling and handfuls of freshly sliced strawberries, this Swiss roll is what we'd call English summertime on a plate. Serve this one with edible flowers or share with friends from a paper plate at your local park – you won't regret it.

EQUIPMENT

40 x 30cm Swiss roll tin

non-stick baking parchment

electric hand whisk

1 Preheat the oven to 200°C/fan 180°C/gas 6. Grease and line the Swiss roll tin with baking parchment.

2 In a large mixing bowl whisk together the eggs and caster sugar for about 5 minutes until the mixture is very thick and pale. Lift the whisk out of the mixture and move it across the bowl to check that the trail it leaves keeps its shape for a few seconds.

3 Sift the flour over the cake batter and gently fold it in until it is fully incorporated. Pour the batter into the tin, carefully level the surface, then bake it in the oven for 10–12 minutes until it is just firm to the touch and golden brown.

INGREDIENTS

butter, for greasing

3 large eggs

100g caster sugar, plus extra for sprinkling

100g plain flour

FOR THE FILLING AND DRIZZLE

200ml double cream

50ml Baileys, plus 1 tbsp

200g strawberries

40g milk chocolate

4) While the sponge cooks put a large sheet of baking parchment on a wire cooling rack and lightly sprinkle it with caster sugar. Remove the tin from the oven and tip the sponge on to the sugar-coated parchment. Carefully peel the baking parchment from the base of the sponge, then roll it up from one short edge and leave it to cool.

5) For the filling, whisk the double cream until soft peaks form, add 50ml of Baileys and whisk again. Hull the strawberries then slice them thinly.

6) Carefully unroll the Swiss roll and spread the cream over it in an even layer. Top with the strawberry slices and roll it up again. Place it on a serving plate.

7) For the drizzle, melt the milk chocolate and 1 tablespoon of Baileys in a bowl, on a low heat in a microwave or over a pan of gently simmering water, until you have a smooth sauce. Drizzle this over the Swiss roll and leave it to set before cutting the cake into slices and serving. This is best eaten on the day it is baked, in the fresh air and with a summer soundtrack playing in the background.

Try This

Replace the strawberry slices with lemon curd: spread the curd over the sponge, top with cream and roll up the sponge. Dust with extra caster sugar instead of the chocolate drizzle.

'You Deserve It'
CHAI LATTE

Life's too short not to enjoy this indulgent, creamy chai latte. The spices will carry you far from the everyday, so even at the height of summer this relaxing drink is exactly what you'll need in your life.

EQUIPMENT

small frying pan
milk frother

INGREDIENTS

1 cinnamon stick
4 cardamom pods, split
2 cloves
3 peppercorns
1cm piece fresh
    ginger, sliced
2 teabags
250ml milk
2 tbsp Baileys
ground cinnamon,
    to serve

1) In a small frying pan, dry fry the spices and ginger slices for a couple of minutes to release their aromas. Put them in a teapot or cafetiere along with the teabags and pour over 250ml boiling water. Leave everything to infuse for 10 minutes.

2) Heat the milk in a small pan or milk frother until it is just simmering, then froth until it's foamy. Strain the chai infusion into your two best mugs, stir a tablespoon of Baileys into each and top them with the frothy milk. Dust the top with a little ground cinnamon and serve immediately, letting the spices warm you all the way through.

Playful
BROWNIE BITES

COOKING TIME
20 MINS

MAKES
40

PREP TIME
20 MINS

A recipe designed to help you live your most delicious life. Pop one (or a few) of these in your mouth in one go, or just serve with ice-cream for a mini-sundae – that's really tasty, too.

EQUIPMENT

32 x 22cm baking tin

non-stick baking parchment

electric hand whisk

INGREDIENTS

200g butter, plus extra for greasing

300g dark chocolate, broken into chunks

100ml Baileys

225g caster sugar

4 large eggs

220g plain flour

1) Preheat the oven to 180°C/fan 160°C/gas 4. Grease and line the baking tin with baking parchment.

2) Put the butter, chocolate and Baileys in a bowl and melt them either in the microwave or over a pan of gently simmering water. Stir to combine the ingredients until all the chocolate chunks have melted. Remove the bowl and set aside.

3) In a large bowl whisk the sugar and eggs until they are pale and thick, then add the chocolate and butter mixture and whisk again. Add the flour and fold it in until fully incorporated, then pour the mixture into the prepared tin.

4) Bake the brownie in the oven for 20 minutes until it is firm to the touch and the surface is starting to crack. Leave it to cool for 10 minutes in the tin, then transfer it to a wire rack and leave it to cool completely.

5) Cut the brownie into 40 small squares and store them in an airtight container. Enjoy with an iced coffee in the sun, or as a picnic pudding.

PANNA COTTA

Prepping time
15 MINS

SERVES 4

Cool, creamy and fresh, this classy dessert shows off the sophisticated side of Baileys. Serve at the end of a long, lazy garden lunch or for the grand finale of an outdoor dinner on a warm, starry evening.

EQUIPMENT

4 x 150ml pudding moulds

INGREDIENTS

sunflower oil, for greasing
3 small gelatine leaves
100ml Baileys
450ml double cream
50g golden caster sugar
sliced strawberries, to serve

Try This

Serve with a summer fruit coulis made from fresh raspberries or strawberries – mash and sieve the berries, then mix them with a little icing sugar to taste.

1. Lightly grease the inside of the pudding moulds with a little oil, then wipe away any excess with a piece of kitchen paper so they are not too oily.

2. Soak the gelatine leaves in a bowl of cold water for 5 minutes to soften them. Heat the Baileys, cream and sugar in a small pan until the sugar dissolves. Remove the pan from the heat, then squeeze out each gelatine leaf separately and add it to the pan, stirring well between each leaf to ensure they all melt.

3. Divide the mixture between the four pudding moulds and leave it to cool before putting them in the fridge. Cool for 3–4 hours to set completely.

4. Run a small, round-bladed knife around the top edge of the moulds and turn out each panna cotta on a small plate. If they don't come out straight away dip each mould in a bowl of hot water for about 10 seconds and try again. Giving the mould a little shake as you hold it over the plate will also help the panna cotta come out. Decorate with sliced strawberries for a beautiful plate of summery deliciousness.

Spiced
COLD BREW

The time has finally come. SUMMER! So, why not give your ordinary cold brew the glow-up it deserves? All you need do is mix it up with cream and spice, then it's ready for ice. Now for the last (and possibly most important) step. Find a perfect spot in the sunshine to sip and indulge.

INGREDIENTS

60ml Baileys

45ml cold brew or cold espresso coffee

1 tbsp cinnamon syrup

ice

1. In a jug whisk together the Baileys, coffee and cinnamon syrup until combined.

2. Fill a glass with ice, generously pour over the coffee mixture and serve immediately, enjoying the refreshing coolness of your summer treat.

Strawberry
DAIQUIRI

Did someone say cocktail hour?
A rich, fruity drink that's simple
and classy, this daiquiri gives
a Baileys lift to the traditional
recipe. Decorate with a couple
of straws and as many mini
umbrellas as your heart desires
for some serious holiday vibes.

EQUIPMENT

blender

balloon or coupe glass

INGREDIENTS

175g strawberries

50ml Baileys

4 ice cubes

1. Hull the strawberries and whizz them in the blender until you have a smooth purée.

2. Add the Baileys and the ice cubes, then whizz again until you have a thick and creamy drink.

3. Splash into a balloon or coupe glass and serve immediately, decorated with a strawberry, and enjoy on a reclining chair.

Opulent
PROFITEROLES

These delicious mini-puffs are so moreish it's almost (make that definitely) impossible to have just a few – add a Baileys filling and Baileys chocolate sauce and you'll just have to give in to the indulgence (see photo overleaf).

(see photo overleaf)

EQUIPMENT

2 baking sheets

non-stick baking parchment

2 piping bags

1.5cm plain nozzle

electric hand whisk

1cm plain nozzle

1) Preheat the oven to 200°C/ fan 180°C/gas 6. Line each baking sheet with baking parchment.

2) For the profiteroles, put the butter and sugar in a pan with 200ml of water and heat them gently over a low heat until the butter melts. Increase the heat and bring the mixture to the boil, then remove the pan from the heat, tip in all the flour and beat the mixture with a wooden spoon until it is smooth. Return the pan to a medium heat and cook for 1–2 minutes, stirring constantly, until the dough starts to come away from the sides of the pan. Remove the pan from the heat again and leave the mixture to cool slightly.

3) Add the egg to the dough a little at a time, beating well between each addition with a wooden spoon. The dough should be glossy and smooth with a soft dropping consistency.

INGREDIENTS

75g butter

1 tsp caster sugar

100g plain flour

3 medium eggs,
   lightly beaten

FOR THE FILLING

300ml double cream

3 tbsp icing sugar

3 tbsp Baileys

FOR THE CHOCOLATE SAUCE

150ml double cream

100g dark chocolate,
   broken into chunks

1 tbsp golden syrup

3 tbsp Baileys

4. Spoon the dough into the piping bag fitted with the 1.5cm nozzle and pipe walnut-sized rounds on to the baking parchment, leaving a 2cm gap between each one.

5. Bake the profiteroles in the oven for 20–25 minutes until they are golden brown and crisp. Allow them to cool for a couple of minutes on the baking sheets, then cut a small slit in the side of each one and leave them to cool completely on a wire rack. The slit allows the steam to escape and stops the profiteroles from going soggy as they cool.

6. For the filling, whisk the cream and icing sugar together until soft peaks form, then slowly add the Baileys and whisk again. Fit the second piping bag with the 1cm nozzle, fill it with cream and pipe the cream into the profiteroles through the slits in the sides.

7. For the chocolate sauce, put the cream, chocolate, syrup and Baileys into a small pan over a gentle heat. Stir occasionally until the chocolate melts and you have a thick glossy sauce. Pour the sauce into a jug.

8. Serve the Baileys-filled profiteroles with the glossy chocolate sauce poured over the top and eat them immediately — if not sooner. Total pleasure.

Luscious RIPPLE ICE-CREAM

Nothing says summer like a delicious Baileys ice-cream – cool and dreamy, and good for demolishing in the sun. And not only does this treat have an amazing flavour, but the bright-pink ripples really do look as good as they taste – that's a fact (see photo on previous page).

INGREDIENTS

400ml full-fat milk

1 vanilla pod, split lengthways

4 large egg yolks

150g caster sugar

400ml double cream

200g raspberries

50ml Baileys

1. Heat the milk and vanilla pod in a pan over a low heat until it just starts to simmer. In a bowl whisk together the egg yolks and 120g of the sugar until they are pale and thick, then slowly add the warmed milk, whisking as you pour. Once all the milk has been incorporated pour the mixture back into the pan.

2. Heat gently for about 10 minutes until the mixture thickens: it should be thick enough to coat the back of a spoon and when you draw your finger through the custard on the spoon it should leave a clean trail. Remove the pan from the heat, pour the mixture back into the bowl and leave it to cool.

3. Once the mixture is completely cold, remove the vanilla pod, pour the custard into a shallow, lidded plastic container and freeze it for an hour. Remove the ice-cream from the freezer and beat it with a wooden spoon to break up the ice crystals, then return it to the freezer for another hour.

4. Whisk the cream until soft peaks form. Scrape the ice-cream into a bowl, beat it again, then fold in the whipped cream and return it to the plastic container to freeze for another hour.

5. Mash the raspberries in a bowl with the remaining 30g of sugar then pass them through a sieve and stir in the Baileys. Pop the purée in the freezer for 30 minutes.

6. Remove the raspberry purée and ice-cream from the freezer and spoon the purée into the ice-cream, swirling the two together to create a ripple effect. Return the ice-cream to the freezer and leave it overnight until it is completely frozen.

7. Remove the ice-cream from the freezer and leave it for 10 minutes before scooping. Serve in cones or in your favourite brightly coloured small bowl, and enjoy in the warmth of the day.

Try This

You could use this ice-cream in the sundae on page 58 in place of vanilla ice-cream.

CRÈME BRÛLÉE

Tap-tap-tap. The sound of a spoon on the hardened caramel topping of this classic French dessert, breaking into burnt-sugar shards that mingle with the rich and velvety Baileys custard below ... *Tempted yet?*

EQUIPMENT

electric hand whisk
6 x 150ml ramekins
roasting tin
blowtorch

INGREDIENTS

300ml double cream
200ml full-fat milk
1 vanilla pod, split, or
   1 tsp vanilla extract
300ml Baileys
6 large egg yolks
30g caster sugar, plus
   6 tsp for the topping

1) Fill the kettle with water, bring it to the boil and then set it aside. Preheat the oven to 160°C/fan 140°C/gas 3.

2) Heat the cream and milk with the vanilla pod or extract until the mixture is hot but not boiling. Take the pan off the heat and stir in the Baileys.

3) Whisk the egg yolks and 30g of sugar until they are pale and thick. Gradually pour in the Baileys mixture, whisking as you pour. Pour the custard into a mixing jug.

4) Put the ramekins in a roasting tin, divide the custard between them, then pour the boiled water into the tin so it comes two-thirds of the way up the sides of the dishes.

5) Bake the ramekins for 25 minutes until the brûlées are set but still have a slight wobble in the middle. Remove the ramekins from the roasting tin and leave them to cool, then chill them in the fridge for 2 hours to set.

6) Just before serving sprinkle a teaspoon of caster sugar over each ramekin and then heat the sugar with the blowtorch until it has melted and is bubbling and deep golden brown. Do not put the ramekins back in the fridge once you've caramelised the sugar or it will soften. Serve, and enjoy the cracking around the table as everyone digs in to this timeless, decadent pleasure.

Baileys
AUTUMN

~~~~~

Nothing needs a pick-me-up like autumn – the nights are drawing in, the scarves and gloves are coming out and we need something a little more indulgent on these blowy, damp days. So come in from an invigorating walk in the leaves, shake off your boots and dig into the Comforting Banana Bread (like a hug from your fave person – see page 86), or, if you need a quick treat to bring the feeling back into your fingers, our delicious Warming Mug Cake (see page 106). Damn, that's good! And if it's time for a cosy cocktail, we have to recommend the rich Alexander Cocktail (see page 108), the pudding in a glass you know you deserve.

~~~~~

Indulgent
STICKY PUDDING

COOKING TIME
40 MINS

SERVES 8

PREP TIME
30 MINS

Is there a more comforting, warming pud than sticky toffee pudding? We think not. And when you add a Baileys twist ... trust us, it's a crowd-pleaser and just the thing for cosy autumnal get-togethers.

EQUIPMENT

20cm deep square cake tin

non-stick baking parchment

electric hand whisk

INGREDIENTS

100g butter, softened, plus extra for greasing

160g Medjool dates, roughly chopped

50ml Baileys

150g dark brown sugar

2 large eggs, lightly beaten

175g self-raising flour

1 tsp bicarbonate of soda

FOR THE SAUCE

100g butter

175g light muscovado sugar

150ml double cream

50ml Baileys

1. Grease and line the cake tin with baking parchment. Preheat the oven to 180°C/fan 160°C/gas 4.

2. Put the dates and Baileys into a small pan with 100ml water, bring the water to the boil and simmer for 5 minutes. Remove the pan from the heat and set aside.

3. Whisk together the butter and sugar until they are pale and fluffy. Add the beaten egg a little at a time, beating well between each addition. Sift the flour and bicarbonate of soda over the creamed mixture and gently fold them in. Add the dates along with any liquid in the pan and fold again.

4. Pour the mixture into the cake tin and bake it for 35–40 minutes until it is well risen and golden brown. Check that a skewer inserted in the middle comes out clean. Leave it to cool in the tin for 10 minutes.

5. Meanwhile make the sauce. Put the butter, sugar and cream into a small pan and heat gently until the butter has melted and the sugar dissolved. Bubble for 2–3 minutes to thicken slightly, add the Baileys and heat again, then remove the pan from the heat.

6. Cut the sponge into eight pieces and serve them with a spoonful of sauce poured over the top. Enjoy at the table, or curled up on the comfiest sofa.

Melting Middle PUDDING

COOKING TIME
40 MINS

SERVES
6

PREP TIME
20 MINS

Sumptuous and rich, this melting-middle pudding is feel-good pleasure in a baking dish, and simple enough that it can be enjoyed on any autumn day.

EQUIPMENT

1½ litre deep baking dish

electric hand whisk

INGREDIENTS

75g butter, softened, plus extra for greasing

110g caster sugar

3 large eggs, separated

60g self-raising flour

50g cocoa powder

325ml full-fat milk

75ml Baileys

1) Grease the baking dish and preheat the oven to 180°C/fan 160°C/gas 4.

2) Whisk together the butter and sugar until they are pale and fluffy, then add the egg yolks one at a time, beating well between each addition. Beat in the flour and cocoa powder, then fold in the milk and Baileys.

3) In another bowl whisk the egg whites until they are stiff. Mix a large spoonful into the pudding mixture to loosen it, then fold in the remaining egg whites. Pour the mixture into the greased baking dish.

4) Bake the pudding in the oven for 35–40 minutes until it is well risen, but still has a slight wobble in the middle. Serve immediately in bowls, and get stuck in.

STUFFED PANCAKES

Why wait until Pancake Day? Stuffed full of everything that feels good on a drizzly autumn day – bananas, brown sugar, chocolate, Baileys – these are the perfect weekend brunch treat.

EQUIPMENT

electric hand whisk

20cm non-stick frying pan

30cm frying pan

non-stick baking parchment

INGREDIENTS

100g plain flour

1 large egg

250ml full-fat milk

vegetable oil, for frying

FOR THE FILLING

40g butter

4 bananas, peeled and sliced

3 tbsp light brown sugar

3 tbsp Baileys

FOR THE SAUCE

3 tbsp chocolate sauce

2 tbsp Baileys

1. Put the flour into a mixing bowl and make a well in the centre. In a jug whisk together the egg and milk, then slowly pour into the well, whisking, until fully incorporated. Return to the jug and rest for 30 minutes.

2. Pour oil into the smaller pan, remove any excess with kitchen paper, then heat over a medium heat. Pour in a thin layer of batter and swirl for an even covering. Cook for 1 minute until lightly golden, then turn over and cook for a further minute.

3. Remove and keep warm while you cook the rest of the pancakes. Separate the stack with baking parchment.

4. For the filling, melt the butter in the large frying pan and cook the banana for a couple of minutes until just softening, then sprinkle with sugar. Turn over and cook for 1 minute. Pour over the Baileys, bring it to a simmer, then remove from the heat.

5. To make the sauce, mix the chocolate sauce with the Baileys.

6. Divide the banana mixture between the pancakes and fold each into a triangle. Serve two pancakes each, drizzled with chocolate sauce. Eat immediately.

Comforting
BANANA BREAD

COOKING TIME
1 HOUR

SERVES
8–10

PREP TIME
15 MINS

This banana bread recipe is like a sweet, warm hug, with an extra-special Baileys icing to top it off. Indulge at home or slice it up and take it with you on an autumnal walk.

EQUIPMENT

900g loaf tin

non-stick baking parchment

electric hand whisk

INGREDIENTS

150g butter, softened, plus extra for greasing

150g golden caster sugar

2 large eggs, lightly beaten

200g self-raising flour

3 bananas

50g natural yoghurt

25ml Baileys

FOR THE DRIZZLE

40g icing sugar

1 tbsp Baileys

1) Grease the loaf tin and line it with baking parchment. Preheat the oven to 180°C/fan 160°C/gas 4.

2) Whisk together the butter and sugar until they are pale and fluffy. Whisk in the beaten egg a little at a time, beating well between each addition. Fold the flour into the mixture.

3) Peel and mash the bananas with a fork, then mix in the yoghurt and Baileys. Fold them into the cake mixture until everything is just combined. Pour the mixture into the loaf tin and bake it for about an hour until it is well risen and golden and a skewer inserted in the middle comes out clean. Check the bread after 50 minutes and if the top is becoming too brown loosely cover it with a piece of baking parchment.

4) Leave the banana bread to cool for ten minutes in the tin before removing it to a wire cooling rack to cool completely.

5) For the drizzle, mix together the icing sugar and Baileys and use a teaspoon to drizzle this over the cooled loaf, allowing it to drip down the sides deliciously. Leave the drizzle to set, then slice and share the loaf (or store it in an airtight container for up to four days).

Toasted ALMOND CLUSTERS

COOKING TIME 12 MINS

MAKES 12

PREP TIME 15 MINS

These nutty little clusters are tiny mouthfuls of heaven – perfect for sharing around or keeping all to yourself (we're not judging). Plus, check out the tips opposite for some delicious variations.

EQUIPMENT

2 baking sheets

non-stick baking parchment

INGREDIENTS

100g blanched almonds, chopped into small pieces

50g dried apricots, chopped into small chunks

50g flaked almonds, broken into pieces

50g butter

50g light muscovado sugar

2 tbsp Baileys

25g plain flour

100g dark chocolate

Try This

Replace the blanched almonds with blanched hazelnuts, the apricots with dried cranberries and make as above. Coat the clusters with melted white chocolate instead of dark chocolate.

1 Line the baking sheets with baking parchment and preheat the oven to 170°C/fan 150°C/gas 3.

2 Put the chopped almonds and apricots into a bowl and add the flaked almonds.

3 Put the butter and sugar into a small pan over a medium heat until the butter has melted and the sugar dissolved. Stir in the Baileys, remove the pan from the heat and pour the mixture over the apricots and almonds. Stir to combine everything, then sprinkle over the flour and stir again.

4 Use a dessertspoon to spoon 12 rounds on to the baking sheets, leaving a 3cm gap between each to allow them to spread in the oven. Lightly press down each round with the back of the spoon. Bake them for 12 minutes until they are crisp and golden.

5 Leave the clusters to cool for 10–15 minutes on the baking sheets, then place them on a wire rack to cool completely.

6 Melt the chocolate, either in a heatproof bowl over a pan of gently simmering water, or on a medium heat in the microwave. Spread a teaspoonful of chocolate on the flat base of each cluster and leave them upside down to allow the chocolate to set. Store the clusters in an airtight container for up to a week, or just dig in whenever you're passing by.

SERVES
1

PREP TIME
5
MINS

White RUSSIAN

This on-the-rocks cocktail is too good to wait for. Smooth and luxurious, the Baileys and the coffee liqueur combine to make a heavenly concoction that'll have you savouring every sip.

INGREDIENTS

ice cubes

60ml Baileys

30ml coffee liqueur

1 Half-fill a tumbler with ice, pour over the Baileys and then add the coffee liqueur.

2 Stir the cocktail well and serve it immediately. *Za Zdarovje!*

Chocolate TORTE

This rich, flourless torte is just the thing for when the weather and leaves start to turn – the Baileys and dark chocolate is what we'd call the ultimate comfort treat.

What are you waiting for?

EQUIPMENT

22cm springform tin

non-stick baking parchment

electric hand whisk

INGREDIENTS

200g butter, plus extra for greasing

250g dark chocolate

100ml Baileys

6 large eggs, separated

200g light brown muscovado sugar

120g ground almonds

icing sugar, to decorate (optional)

1) Preheat the oven to 180°C/fan 160°C/gas 4. Grease and line the tin with baking parchment.

2) Put the butter, chocolate and Baileys into a heatproof bowl and either set the bowl over a pan of gently simmering water or heat it on medium power in a microwave until the butter and chocolate have melted. Stir well until you have a smooth glossy mix and set it aside.

3) In a large bowl, whisk together the egg yolks and sugar until they are pale, thick and creamy. Add the chocolate mixture and whisk again until just combined.

4) Clean the beaters and whisk the egg whites in another large bowl until they are stiff. Add a large spoonful to the chocolate mix and stir it in to loosen the mixture. Add the rest of the egg whites and gently fold them in along with the ground almonds.

5) Spoon the mixture into the tin, level the surface and bake for 35–40 minutes until the torte is well risen and firm to the touch, but still has a slight wobble in the middle.

6) Remove the tin from the oven and leave to cool completely in the tin on a wire rack. Dust with icing sugar (if using), remove from the tin and cut into small slices to serve — or, if you prefer, large slices (depending on your day).

Extra-Special
BAILEYS AFFOGATO

What do you get when you combine smooth Baileys, espresso and indulgent vanilla ice-cream? The most delish affogato under the sun, that's what. The perfect 'wow-factor' ending to leisurely weekend brunches with your besties. You can thank us later.

INGREDIENTS

2 scoops vanilla
   ice-cream

30ml Baileys

1 shot hot espresso
   coffee

1 Put the scoops of ice-cream into a small bowl and pour over the Baileys.

2 Pour the hot espresso shot over the top and serve the affogato immediately before the ice-cream melts. A simple but mouthwatering pleasure.

Salted Caramel
BAILEYS COCKTAIL

Is there anything more dreamy than salted caramel? It's hard to try this delicious, creamy cocktail and not think it's a flavour of the gods. And any drink that comes with a cube of fudge on the side has got to be worth trying, right?

EQUIPMENT

cocktail shaker

martini or coupe glass

INGREDIENTS

50ml Baileys

25ml coffee liqueur

15ml vodka

15ml caramel syrup

handful of ice cubes

sea salt flakes and
    salted caramel
    fudge, to decorate

1) Measure the Baileys, coffee liqueur, vodka and caramel syrup into a cocktail shaker and add the ice cubes. Seal the cocktail shaker and shake it vigorously.

2) Strain the cocktail into a martini or coupe glass, sprinkle sea salt flakes over the centre and push a cube of fudge on to the rim of the glass.

3) Serve immediately, and luxuriate in your salty, caramel delight.

Scrumptious
BIRTHDAY CAKE

A big birthday needs a big cake, and since every birthday is big, this is the perfect recipe – delicious, playful and truly, truly scrumptious. Don't skimp on the sprinkles for the essential edible celebration (see photo overleaf).

EQUIPMENT

3 x 20cm sandwich tins

non-stick baking parchment

electric hand whisk

1) Line the sandwich tins with baking parchment and preheat the oven to 180°C/fan 160°C/gas 4.

2) Sift the flour, bicarbonate of soda, baking powder and cocoa powder into a large mixing bowl and stir in the caster sugar. In a jug whisk together the eggs, syrup, oil, milk and Baileys. Pour the liquid mixture into the bowl and whisk it into the dry ingredients until they are fully combined.

3) Divide the mixture between the three cake tins. You can weigh the tins once they are filled to make sure that you have three equal-sized layers. Bake them for 25–30 minutes until they are well risen and a skewer inserted in the centre comes out clean. Leave them to cool for 10 minutes in the tins, then remove them to wire cooling racks to cool completely.

COOKING TIME
30 MINS

SERVES
16–20

PREP TIME
40 MINS

INGREDIENTS

270g plain flour

1½ tsp bicarbonate of soda

1½ tsp baking powder

3 tbsp cocoa powder

210g caster sugar

3 large eggs

3 tbsp golden syrup

180ml corn oil

100ml full-fat milk

80ml Baileys

FOR THE ICING

200g butter, softened

560g icing sugar

50ml Baileys

hundreds and thousands or star-shaped sprinkles, to decorate

4) For the icing, whisk the butter and add the icing sugar a few spoonfuls at a time, beating well between each addition. Beat in the Baileys then the cocoa powder and continue beating until you have a smooth and fluffy buttercream.

5) Place one of the sponges on a cake plate, top with a quarter of the buttercream and use a round-bladed knife to spread it into a smooth layer. Repeat with the other two sponges, putting the top sponge base-up to make sure the top of the cake is flat.

6) Cover the sides and top of the cake with the remaining buttercream and make it as even and smooth as possible. Decorate with hundreds and thousands, as many as you can fit on, plus all the candles you need. Light them up, blow them out, and enjoy! (You can store the cake in an airtight tin for three or four days.)

Mint
MERINGUE GATEAU

This gateau makes a gorgeous autumn recipe, layering three delicate meringues with Baileys cream and dark chocolate. Simple but oh-so-delicious. And don't worry if the meringues aren't perfect – it's the cracks that hold all the flavour ... (See photo on previous page.)

(See photo on previous page.)

EQUIPMENT

non-stick baking parchment
3 baking sheets
electric hand whisk
piping bag with 1cm plain nozzle

1 Draw a 20cm diameter circle on three pieces of baking parchment. Place one piece on each baking sheet with the circle face down. Preheat the oven to 120°C/fan 100°C/gas ½.

2 Put the egg whites into a large bowl and whisk them until stiff peaks form. Add the sugar a spoonful at a time, whisking well between each addition. Add the peppermint extract and the food colouring with the last of the sugar, using enough colouring to give you a pale green mixture.

3 Fit the nozzle to the piping bag and fill the bag with the whisked egg whites. Starting from the centre of a circle,

INGREDIENTS

4 large egg whites

220g caster sugar

1 tsp peppermint extract

green food colouring gel

400ml double cream

100ml Baileys

25g dark chocolate

pipe concentric rings on to each of the drawn circles on the baking sheets.

4) Bake the meringues in the oven for 1 hour until they are firm and crisp. Turn off the oven, prop open the oven door a crack and leave them to cool. Remove them from the oven and allow them to cool completely before removing them from the baking parchment.

5) Whisk the cream until soft peaks form, add the Baileys and whisk again. Place one of the meringue circles on a serving plate and spoon a third of the cream on top. Gently spread it into an even layer. Grate a little chocolate over the cream. Top with another layer of meringue and cream. Swirl the last of the cream on the top layer and use a vegetable peeler to scrape shavings of chocolate over the cream. Serve immediately, using a cake slice to cut through and reveal the delicious layers within.

6) The meringues can be made in advance and stored in an airtight container for up to a week.

Try This

Rose and white chocolate also combine to make a delicious gateau. Replace the peppermint extract with a teaspoon of rose water and the green food colouring with pink to create a pale pink meringue. Replace the dark chocolate with white chocolate between the layers and sprinkle a few dried rose petals on top along with the white chocolate shavings.

Cosy Peach and Apricot
CRUMBLE

COOKING TIME
45 MINS

SERVES 6

PREP TIME
15 MINS

Try This

Instead of cream serve the crumble with the Baileys custard in the Poached Pears recipe (page 110)

Could anything be cosier than this crumble, packed with fruit the colour of autumn leaves and topped with flaked almonds? Oh yes – adding a big dollop of Baileys cream on the side. Perfect.

EQUIPMENT

25 x 20cm shallow baking dish

INGREDIENTS

420g tin peach slices, drained

420g tin apricot halves, drained

100ml Baileys

100g plain flour

100g ground almonds

100g butter, cut into small pieces

100g golden caster sugar

15g flaked almonds

200ml double cream

1 Preheat the oven to 180°C/fan 160°C/gas 4. Cut the peaches and apricots into bite-size pieces and scatter them over the base of the baking dish. Pour 50ml of the Baileys over them.

2 Mix the flour and almonds in a bowl, add the butter and rub it into the flour mixture with your fingertips until it resembles breadcrumbs. Stir in the sugar and then sprinkle the mixture over the fruit.

3 Bake the crumble for about 45 minutes until the top is golden brown. Add the flaked almonds to the top for the last 5 minutes of the cooking time.

4 Whisk the cream in a bowl until soft peaks form, add the remaining 50ml of Baileys and whisk again. Serve the crumble with a big dollop of cream on the side, and dig in to the warming, fruity flavours.

SERVES
2

COOKING TIME
2–2½
MINS

PREP TIME
10
MINS

Warming
MUG CAKE

The perfect pick-me-up after coming in from autumnal walks, this mug cake is ready in minutes and tastes like heaven in a cup. For the full effect, eat it under a warm blanket for the perfect casual indulgence.

EQUIPMENT

1 large mug

INGREDIENTS

3 tbsp corn oil, plus
extra for greasing

1 medium egg

3 tbsp Baileys

2 tbsp golden syrup

3 tbsp golden
caster sugar

4 tbsp self-raising flour

1½ tbsp white
chocolate chips

1. Grease the inside of a large mug.

2. In a small bowl, beat together the oil, egg, Baileys and syrup with a fork.

3. Add the sugar and flour and beat again, then fold in 1 tablespoon of the chocolate chips. Pour the mixture into the mug and top with the remaining chocolate chips.

4. Bake in a microwave on full power for 2–2½ minutes until the cake is well risen and starting to come away from the sides of the mug. Leave it to cool for 5 minutes then dig in.

Heavenly CHOCOLATE POTS

CHILLING TIME
2–3
HOURS

SERVES
4

PREP TIME
15
MINS

A rich, sumptuous dessert where a little goes a long way. These chocolate pots are a double pleasure with two different types of chocolate, as well as a generous splash of Baileys.

Cloud nine, here we come.

EQUIPMENT

electric hand whisk

4 small glass bowls, ramekins or teacups

INGREDIENTS

50g milk chocolate, broken into chunks

100g dark chocolate, broken into chunks

3 large egg yolks

50g golden caster sugar

200ml double cream

75ml Baileys

1. Melt the milk and dark chocolate chunks in a bowl, either in the microwave or over a pan of gently simmering water. Set it aside to cool slightly.

2. In a large bowl, whisk together the egg yolks and sugar until you have a pale and very thick mixture.

3. In another bowl whisk the cream until soft peaks form, add the Baileys and whisk again.

4. Pour the cooled chocolate on to the egg mixture and fold it in until it is combined. Add the whipped cream and fold again.

5. Spoon the mixture into four beautiful little glass bowls, ramekins or teacups and chill in the fridge for 2–3 hours to set, then serve with a smile and watch everyone polish them off.

ALEXANDER
COCKTAIL

If you like your cocktails to resemble a dessert, then this one's for you. Rich and creamy, this pudding in a glass is your decadent treat for cosy nights next to the fire (even if it's on a screen). So go on, slide into a comfortable robe and put your feet up.

EQUIPMENT

cocktail shaker

martini glass

INGREDIENTS

50ml Baileys

25ml Crème de Cacao

25ml double cream

handful of ice

grated nutmeg,
  to decorate

1. Pour the Baileys and Crème de Cacao into the cocktail shaker and add the cream and the ice. Seal the cocktail shaker tightly and shake it vigorously to combine all the ingredients.

2. Strain the cocktail into a martini glass and decorate it with a little grated nutmeg. Serve immediately, while lounging cosily.

Poached Pears
WITH CREAMY CUSTARD

Feeling a bit sophisticated?
Poached fruit always makes a
stylish pud, and the combination
of spices with pears, and rich
Baileys and vanilla in the custard,
makes this a delectable end to
any autumn meal.

EQUIPMENT

balloon whisk

1) Put the sugar, cinnamon, ginger and lemon zest in a pan
big enough to hold the pears in a single layer. Add a litre
of cold water and heat the pan over a gentle heat until the
sugar dissolves, then increase the heat slightly to bring the
syrup to a simmer.

2) Meanwhile peel the pears, leaving the stalks intact. Trim the
bases slightly so the pears stand upright, and use a teaspoon
to scoop out the core from the base. Place the pears in the
pan of syrup, cover with a lid and simmer them gently for
about an hour or until they are tender – the cooking time
will vary depending on the ripeness of the pears.

INGREDIENTS

250g caster sugar

1 cinnamon stick

2cm piece fresh
   ginger, sliced

1 strip lemon zest

4 pears

FOR THE CUSTARD

75ml Baileys

250ml full-fat milk

2 large egg yolks

30g golden caster sugar

1 tbsp cornflour

1 tsp vanilla extract

3. For the custard, heat the Baileys and milk in a pan until they just start to bubble at the edges. Whisk the egg yolks, sugar and cornflour together in a bowl to form a smooth paste. Slowly add the hot milk and Baileys to the bowl, whisking as you pour. Return the mixture to the pan, then heat over a low heat, stirring constantly until the custard thickens. This will take about 10 minutes. You will know it is ready if you lift the spoon and run your finger through the custard on the back and it leaves a clean trail behind. Once the custard has thickened, add the vanilla extract.

4. When the pears are tender remove them from the pan with a slotted spoon and sit them upright in bowls, then pour over the custard. Be generous with it, and let the pears sit in their golden custard baths for a moment before you finish them off.

Baileys
WINTER

Brrrr! It's cold and dark out there, and any trip into the sleet and snow requires a warming prize for your amazing effort. Bring out your softest blankets and warmest fairy lights and tuck into the winter recipes, sure to be asked for again and again by any of your friends lucky enough to taste them. Enjoy a Christmas treat with our sumptuous festive 'Merry Treatmas' Yule Log (see page 146), toast the New Year with a v extra Baileys Grasshopper (see page 136), bring in some joy with the sprinkled, starry Joyful Cake Pops (see page 130) or snuggle up into full hibernation after a bowl of warming Hyggelig Bread and Butter Pudding (see page 132), the cure for any winter's day. We got you.

'Treat Yourself'
FREAKSHAKE

It's time to treat yo'self! This is like no milkshake you've had before, and the only limit is your imagination. Don't hold back. Garnish your freakshake all the way to irresistibility. More marshmallows! More pretzels! More sprinkles!

EQUIPMENT

blender

electric hand whisk

glass mug or
   sundae glass

INGREDIENTS

2 scoops chocolate
   ice-cream

50ml Baileys, plus 2 tsp

150ml full-fat milk

100ml double cream

chocolate sauce,
   for drizzling

TO DECORATE

marshmallows

chocolate-covered
   pretzels

biscuits of your choice

1. Put the ice-cream, 50ml of the Baileys and the milk into a blender and whizz them to combine.

2. Whisk the double cream until it stands in soft peaks, add the 2 teaspoons of Baileys and whisk again.

3. Pour the milkshake into a glass mug or sundae glass, top with the whipped cream and drizzle over plenty of chocolate sauce.

4. Add some marshmallows, pretzels and biscuits, then drizzle over more sauce – the more the merrier – and serve the freakshake with a straw and a spoon. It's a masterpiece, isn't it? So enjoy!

Try This

Replace the chocolate ice-cream with strawberry ice-cream and the chocolate sauce with caramel sauce and make as above.

Hug-in-a-Mug
VANILLA
HOT CHOCOLATE

Soothing, warming, cheering – this hot chocolate is the perfect treat for when you need something that doesn't just taste good, but looks good too. Sprinkles, flakes and stroopwafels? Yes please!

EQUIPMENT

electric hand whisk or balloon whisk

INGREDIENTS

400ml full-fat milk

½ tsp vanilla bean paste or vanilla extract

120g white chocolate, chopped into small pieces

100ml Baileys

150ml double cream

TO DECORATE

2 mini cookies or mini stroopwafels

2 tsp white chocolate flakes

2 tsp metallic coloured sprinkles

1. Heat the milk in small pan with the vanilla until it is just simmering – but don't let it boil. Add the chocolate and stir until it has melted.

2. Add the Baileys and once it is warmed through remove the pan from the heat.

3. Whip the cream until soft peaks form.

4. Divide the hot chocolate between two mugs, top them with the whipped cream and push the cookies or stroopwafels into the cream. Sprinkle over the chocolate flakes and sprinkles. An essential hug in a mug.

Mud
SLIDE

When winter weather makes it seem like there's more mud than paths outside, maybe it's time to come indoors, get into something comfy and enjoy a classic cocktail with a Baileys twist.

EQUIPMENT

cocktail shaker

martini glass

INGREDIENTS

50ml Baileys

15ml Smirnoff
   No. 21 vodka

handful of ice cubes

1 tsp chocolate sauce

1) Pour the Baileys and vodka into the cocktail shaker and add the ice. Seal the shaker and and shake it vigorously until all the ingredients are well mixed and chilled.

2) Swirl the chocolate sauce around the inside of a martini glass, strain the cocktail into the glass and serve it immediately. Here's mud in your eye!

Decadent
S'MORES

Our (indoor) take on this iconic campfire treat is as s'moreish as you can get. Decadent and deliciously gooey, they're the perfect comforting treat, any day of the week.

EQUIPMENT

2 ramekins or jars
blowtorch

INGREDIENTS

4 shortbread biscuits, crumbled
75ml Baileys
2 tbsp chocolate sauce
4 large marshmallows
handful of mini marshmallows

1. Divide the crumbled biscuits between the ramekins.

2. Heat the Baileys and chocolate sauce until they are smooth, either in a small pan over a gentle heat or in the microwave.

3. Divide the mini marshmallows between the two ramekins, then pour over the warmed chocolate and Baileys sauce. Top each ramekin with 2 large marshmallows. Heat these with a blowtorch until they are golden and start to melt.

4. Serve immediately. Ready, steady, dig in! Last one to finish does the washing up.

Rich & Fruity
BAILEYS TRIFLE

This creamy bowl of heaven is super quick, super easy and super delicious. Take a big spoonful of Baileys custard, cake and berries and celebrate another perfect day for trifle.

EQUIPMENT

balloon whisk

INGREDIENTS

FOR THE CUSTARD
100ml Baileys
500ml full-fat milk
4 large egg yolks
60g caster sugar
2 tbsp cornflour

275g madeira cake
100ml Baileys
500g frozen berries, defrosted
600ml double cream
sprinkles, to decorate

1 First make the custard: heat the Baileys and milk in a pan until it just starts to bubble at the edges. Whisk the egg yolks, sugar and cornflour together in a mixing bowl with a balloon whisk to form a smooth paste. Slowly add the hot milk and Baileys to the bowl, whisking as your pour.

2 Return the mix to the pan, then heat over a low heat, stirring constantly until the custard thickens; this will take about 10 minutes. You know the custard is ready when you lift the spoon from the pan and run your finger through the custard on the back of the spoon and a clean trail is left behind. Pour the custard back into the bowl and cover the surface with a piece of cling film to prevent a skin forming. Set aside to cool.

3. Cut the madeira cake into 2cm thick slices and place in the base of your trifle dish. Pour over the Baileys and set aside to soak for 10 minutes. Spoon the defrosted berries on top of the sponge then pour over the cooled custard.

4. Place in the fridge for 1 hour to chill completely – to allow the flavours to develop fully you can chill overnight and finish off the next day.

5. With a balloon whisk, whip the cream until soft peaks are formed, then gently spoon billowy mounds on top of the trifle and add the sprinkles to finish. Ta-dah! Who needs serving bowls when you can just dig right in?

Try This

For the flavour of the Black Forest, replace the Madeira cake with chocolate cake and the frozen berries with Black Forest frozen fruits or frozen cherries, then top with grated dark chocolate instead of sprinkles.

Black Forest
GATEAU CUPCAKES

These cupcakes – like a miniature, scrumptious snowy forest – are almost too pretty to eat. But they taste as good as they look, so we guarantee you won't be able to resist digging in.

EQUIPMENT

12-hole muffin tin
paper muffin cases
electric hand whisk

INGREDIENTS

8 chocolate muffins
6 tbsp cherry or
   raspberry jam
24 fresh or tinned
   pitted cherries
400ml double cream
75ml Baileys
1 chocolate flake,
   broken into 12 pieces

1. Line the muffin tin with the cases. Cut each muffin into three horizontally so you have 24 circular slices of sponge. Place a slice in the bottom of each paper case – use the smallest slices for this.

2. Set aside 1 tablespoon of the jam and divide the remainder between the cases. Cut 12 cherries in half and put two pieces on top of each layer of jam. Add a second slice of sponge to each muffin case and press it down gently.

3. Whip the cream until soft peaks form, add the Baileys and whisk again. Spoon some cream on top of each cupcake. Sift the remaining tablespoon of jam and thin with a little syrup if you are using tinned cherries, or water if the cherries are fresh. Drizzle over the cream, then top each cake with a whole cherry and a piece of chocolate flake.

4. Carefully remove the laden cases from the muffin tin and serve. Time to indulge!

Feel-Good
BAILEYS FONDUE

This is a warming fondue of Baileys, chocolate, biscuits and fruit – aka the best party food you've ever tasted. It's cosy while also being decadent, like being at a dinner party in a fluffy animal onesie. Bliss.

INGREDIENTS

100g milk chocolate, broken into chunks

100g dark chocolate, broken into chunks

100ml double cream

50ml Baileys

250g strawberries

200g large marshmallows

3 bananas, peeled and sliced

12–18 amaretti biscuits

1. Put the milk and dark chocolate chunks, the cream and the Baileys into a bowl over a pan of gently simmering water, ensuring that the base of the bowl doesn't touch the water. Heat gently until the chocolate has melted, stirring occasionally, until you have a thick glossy sauce.

2. Pour the mixture into a warmed serving dish and place it on a large platter surrounded by the strawberries, marshmallows, banana slices and biscuits for dipping. Serve immediately. Alternatively, if you have a fondue pot you can pour the sauce into that and set the heat to low to keep the chocolate warm for longer. Now, this can be a messy dish and that chocolate might go everywhere, but a little mess never hurt anyone, did it? Particularly when it tastes this good . . .

Volcano
CAKE

Quick, rich and indulgent – the only eruptions this volcano cake will make is the Baileys-and-chocolate flavour bursting in your mouth. (You can pretend the raspberries are lava boulders, though, if it helps ...)

INGREDIENTS

400g chocolate
   brownies

40ml chocolate sauce

50ml Baileys

raspberries, to decorate

1) Stack the brownies on a large plate. Mould them into the shape you want your volcano to be. Remember to leave a hole in the top for the delicious lava.

2) Drizzle over the chocolate sauce, then pour the Baileys into the hole.

3) Arrange the raspberries around the sides of the volcano.

4) Demolish your volcano before it erupts!

Nutterlicious
COCKTAIL

A nutterly tasty cocktail from chocolate heaven – and with bananas, hazelnuts and Baileys too, this might be one best kept for special occasions (like whenever you fancy some pure deliciousness in a glass).

EQUIPMENT

blender

2 cocktail glasses

INGREDIENTS

20g milk chocolate, melted, or 1 tsp chocolate hazelnut spread

60g chopped toasted hazelnuts, plus extra to decorate

100ml Baileys

200ml almond milk

1 banana, peeled and sliced

a few ice cubes

1 Smooth the melted chocolate or a little chocolate hazelnut spread around the rim of the cocktail glasses.

2 Spread most of the chopped hazelnuts on a plate, then dip the rims of the glasses into them. Put the rest of the hazelnuts in a blender with the Baileys, almond milk and banana, add the ice cubes and blend until the mixture is smooth.

3 Pour into the prepared glasses and sprinkle a few chopped hazelnuts over the top. Sip elegantly or slurp through a straw – it's delicious either way.

Joyful
CAKE POPS

An extra-special treat, these small delights are (quite literally) joy on a stick. Decorate with the sprinkles that make you feel most cheerful: green and red, gold and silver, multicoloured stars – you do you!

EQUIPMENT

electric hand whisk

16 thin lolly sticks

INGREDIENTS

375g Madeira cake

50ml Baileys

75g butter, softened

150g icing sugar

250g white chocolate, broken into chunks

sprinkles, to decorate

1) In a large bowl crumble the cake until it resembles breadcrumbs. Pour over the Baileys and leave it to soak into the cake crumbs.

2) In another bowl beat the butter and icing sugar until they are light and fluffy. Stir this buttercream through the cake crumbs, then divide the mixture into 16 pieces and roll each piece into a ball.

3) Push a lolly stick into each ball and put the balls in the fridge to set for at least an hour.

4) Melt the chocolate in a bowl over a pan of gently simmering water or in the microwave on a medium heat. Take the cake balls out of the fridge. Remove the lolly sticks from the cakes one by one and dip each stick into the melted chocolate, then put it back in the cake (this helps the sticks to stay in place). Next dip each cake ball into the melted chocolate and top it with sprinkles.

5) Set the cakes aside to set, then enjoy biting through their sprinkled chocolate shells and into the soft, sweet insides – or keep them in an airtight container for up to five days.

Hyggelig
BREAD AND
BUTTER PUDDING

COOKING TIME 45 MINS

SERVES 8

PREP TIME 15 MINS

The most *hyggelig* – cosy, snug and soothing – dessert out there, our Baileys bread and butter pudding is simple, but oh-so-scrumptious. Full of juicy sultanas, soft baked bread and a rich Baileys custard, it's the perfect comfort food.

EQUIPMENT

26 x 20cm ovenproof baking dish

electric hand whisk

INGREDIENTS

50g butter, softened, plus extra for greasing

8 slices of day-old, medium-sliced white bread

80g golden caster sugar

80g sultanas

2 large eggs

400ml full-fat milk

200ml Baileys

1 Grease the baking dish with a little of the softened butter.

2 Remove the crusts from the bread, spread the slices with butter and cut each slice into four triangles. Lay half the triangles in the bottom of the baking dish, overlapping them slightly to create an even layer. Scatter over half the sugar and sultanas, then top with the remaining bread and the rest of the sugar and sultanas.

3 In a jug beat together the eggs, milk and Baileys and pour the mixture into the baking dish. Ensure that you pour some mixture over all the bread triangles. Leave the dish to rest for 1–4 hours.

4 Preheat the oven to 180°C/fan 160°C/gas 4. Bake the pudding for 40–45 minutes until the top is golden. Remove from the oven and leave it to stand for 10 minutes before serving, warm, with some seasonal cheer.

RICE PUDDING
with Sumptuous Custard

COOKING TIME
2
HOURS

SERVES
8

PREP TIME
20
MINS

Every wintery walk deserves rice pudding at the end of it, and this one comes with an extra-decadent Baileys custard on top. You'll be speed-walking back to enjoy this indulgent dessert.

EQUIPMENT

ovenproof baking dish

balloon whisk

INGREDIENTS

100g pudding rice

500ml full-fat milk

500ml double cream

200ml Baileys

50g caster sugar

100g sultanas

25g butter

FOR THE CUSTARD

75ml Baileys

250ml full-fat milk

2 large egg yolks

30g golden caster sugar

1 tbsp cornflour

1 Preheat the oven to 150°C/fan 130°C/gas 2. Put the rice in an ovenproof dish, pour over the milk, cream and Baileys and stir, then add the sugar and sultanas and stir again. Cut the butter into small pieces and dot them over the top.

2 Bake the pudding for 30 minutes then give it a stir and bake for a further 1½ hours until it is thickened and bubbling.

3 Meanwhile make the custard. Heat the Baileys and milk in a pan until it bubblea at the edges. Whisk the egg yolks, sugar and cornflour in a mixing bowl to a smooth paste. Slowly add the hot milk and Baileys, whisking as you pour.

4 Return the mixture to the pan, then heat over a low heat, stirring constantly until the custard thickens – about 10 minutes. The custard is ready when you can lift the spoon from the pan and run your finger through the custard on the back of the spoon so it leaves a clean trail behind.

5 Serve the rice pudding, with the sumptuous custard in a thick jug to be generously poured over each serving. Guaranteed to warm even the most chilled bones.

Ultimate
TIRAMISU

CHILLING TIME
OVER-
NIGHT

SERVES
8

PREP TIME
20
MINS

Special occasions deserve showstopping desserts, and our tiramisu recipe ticks all the boxes. Decadent? Check. Moreish? Hell, yeah. Comforting? You bet. All you'll need to add to your Christmas table is some festive glamour, your besties and a bucketful of cheer.

EQUIPMENT

electric hand whisk

25 x 15 x 5cm
baking dish

INGREDIENTS

400ml double cream

250g mascarpone
cheese

50g golden caster sugar

100ml Baileys

250ml freshly brewed
coffee, cooled

175g sponge fingers

15g dark chocolate,
to decorate

1 In a large mixing bowl, whisk together the cream, mascarpone and sugar until they are thick and creamy. Add 50ml of the Baileys and whisk again.

2 Mix together the coffee and the remaining 50ml of Baileys in a shallow bowl. Dip half the sponge fingers in the coffee mixture for a few seconds – long enough to absorb some flavour, but not so long that they collapse – and use them to line the base of the baking dish in a single layer.

3 Spread half the whipped cream mixture over this layer then dip and add the remaining sponge fingers. Pour any leftover coffee over this layer and top it with the rest of the cream.

4 Chill the tiramisu in the fridge for a few hours, or ideally overnight. Finely grate the chocolate over the top just before serving, and spoon out into individual dishes before your happy crowd.

Grasshopper
COCKTAIL

If there's one time of year to be a bit extra, it's the festive season, right? This bright-green cocktail classic with a scrumptious addition of creamy Baileys is bound to get you in the Christmas spirit.

EQUIPMENT

cocktail shaker

martini or coupe glass

INGREDIENTS

50ml Baileys

50ml Crème de Menthe

50ml double cream

handful of ice

dark chocolate, to decorate

mint leaf, to decorate

1 Pour the Baileys and Crème de Menthe into the cocktail shaker, then add the cream and ice. Seal the cocktail shaker tightly and shake it vigorously to combine everything.

2 Strain the cocktail into a martini or coupe glass and decorate it with a little finely grated dark chocolate and a fresh mint leaf. Serve immediately, beneath some glowing festive fairy lights.

Hot CHOCOLATE

There are many ways to warm up in winter, but Baileys hot chocolate with all the toppings is the best.

EQUIPMENT

250ml milk

50ml Baileys

3 tsps hot chocolate powder

squirty cream

dusting of cocoa powder

OPTIONAL EXTRAS

chocolate sprinkles

chocolate brownies

chocolate fingers

chocolate sauce

chocolate anything to garnish!

1 Heat the milk and Baileys in a small pan over a medium heat until just simmering.

2 Add the hot chocolate powder to a mug, pour the hot milk into the mug and stir well until rich and chocolatey.

3 Squirt a generous swirl of cream on top and dust with cocoa powder. Or garnish gregariously: dollop on fresh or whipped cream, marshmallows (toasted marshmallows take it to another level), chocolate flakes, whatever you fancy. Stand back and admire. Then grab a spoon and dig in.

Festive
MINCE PIES WITH BAILEYS BUTTER

What is the holiday season for if not sharing these indulgent mouthfuls of deliciousness? We've all had mince pies, but a warm Baileys mince pie is something else entirely – and with Baileys butter on the side ... *chef's kiss* (see photo overleaf).

EQUIPMENT

rolling pin

fluted pastry cutters

12-hole cupcake/
  bun tin

1   Put the flour in a large mixing bowl and add the butter cubes. Rub the butter into the flour with your fingertips until the mixture resembles breadcrumbs. Stir in the sugar, then add the egg and bring the mixture together to form a soft dough. Add a dash of cold water if necessary. Wrap the pastry in cling film and leave it to chill in the fridge for 30 minutes.

2   Preheat the oven to 200°C/fan 180°C/gas 6. Mix the Baileys into the mincemeat and set it aside.

Try This

Instead of topping the pies with lids, cut 12 stars out of the pastry and top the mince pies with these, brushing them with milk as above before baking.

INGREDIENTS

200g plain flour, plus extra for dusting

100g butter, chilled and cut into cubes

1 tsp caster sugar

1 egg, lightly beaten

1 tbsp Baileys

250g mincemeat

2 tbsp milk, for brushing

FOR THE BAILEYS BUTTER

75g butter, softened

75g icing sugar

2 tbsp Baileys

③ On a lightly-floured surface roll out the pastry to the thickness of a £1 coin and cut out 12 circles large enough to line the holes of your tin. Press them down gently inside the holes using a small ball of pastry. Cut 12 smaller circles for lids from the remaining pastry.

④ Place a teaspoonful of mincemeat in each pie. Brush the underneath edges of each lid with a little milk and place the lids on the top of the pies. Press the edges together lightly to seal them. Brush the top of each pie with a little more milk, then use a small sharp knife to cut a slit in the top of each to allow the steam to escape.

⑤ Bake the mince pies in the oven for 15–20 minutes until they are golden. Leave them to cool in the tin for 5 minutes before carefully removing them to a wire rack to cool completely.

⑥ For the Baileys butter, beat the butter until it is smooth, add the icing sugar and Baileys and beat again. Serve each mince pie on a jolly plate, with a spoonful of the delicious, creamy Baileys butter to warm from the inside out.

'Hell, yeah!'
HOT CHOCOLATE BOMBS

On a cold, dark winter's night, you need more than an ordinary hot chocolate ... Find an extra-large mug and your best festive film, get cosy and savour our indulgent 'Hell, yeah!' hot chocolate bomb – so named because it'll blow your socks off. (See photo on previous page.)

(See photo on previous page.)

EQUIPMENT

2 x 6-hole, half-sphere, 5.5cm chocolate silicone moulds

6 mugs

1. Melt the chocolate in a bowl over a pan of gently simmering water, or on a medium heat in the microwave, until it is completely smooth. Put a teaspoon of chocolate into the six holes in the mould and swirl the chocolate round to completely cover the inside of each mould. Pour any excess chocolate back into the bowl. Scrape any chocolate drips from the flat areas between each hole to ensure that the shapes have clean edges. Repeat with the other mould so you have 12 chocolate halves in total.

2. Place the moulds on a wire rack upside down and leave the chocolate linings to set for 1 hour.

INGREDIENTS

200g milk chocolate, broken into chunks, plus extra for topping

6 tbsp Baileys

36 mini marshmallows, plus extra for serving

1.2 litres milk, to serve (200ml per chocolate bomb)

(3) Repeat the step above, adding a second layer of chocolate on top of the first. Melt the chocolate in the bowl again if necessary, but ensure that it is cool before adding a second layer to the moulds. Again, leave the moulds for a couple of hours to allow the second layer of chocolate to set firm, but do not put them in the fridge or the chocolate will become dull instead of shiny.

(4) Melt the remaining chocolate one more time, spoon it on to a small plate and spread it into an even layer. Gently remove the chocolate bowls from the moulds by turning them upside down and peeling the mould away from them one at a time. Dip the rim of each one into the chocolate on the plate, making sure that the whole rim is covered.

(5) Spoon a tablespoon of Baileys into six of the chocolate bowls, add six mini marshmallows and then top each one with another bowl, matching the edges as neatly as possible. Press the halves together gently to seal the edges and lightly run a fingertip around the seal to make sure that any gaps in the melted chocolate are filled. Leave the bombs for a couple of hours to set.

(6) To serve, heat the milk to simmering point. Place one chocolate bomb in each mug and pour the hot milk over it. Stir to melt the chocolate completely and add extra marshmallows and a little grated milk chocolate to the top. Don your softest socks, snuggle under your favourite blanket, and enjoy the best hot chocolate you'll ever have.

'Merry Treatmas'
BAILEYS YULE LOG

It's the most wonderful time of the year – aka Yule Log season. Whether you love yours dusted with sugar-snow or sprinkled with stars, our recipe is bound to impress whoever's around your Christmas table (see photo overleaf).

EQUIPMENT

40 x 30cm Swiss roll tin

non-stick baking parchment

electric hand whisk

clean tea towel

1) Preheat the oven to 200°C/180°C fan/gas 6. Grease and line the tin with baking parchment.

2) Put the chocolate pieces into a bowl, set it over a pan of gently simmering water and heat gently until the chocolate is melted and smooth, or melt it on a medium heat in the microwave. Set it aside to cool.

3) In a large mixing bowl whisk together the eggs and caster sugar for about 5 minutes until they are very thick and pale. When you lift the beaters out of the mix and move them across the bowl the trail they leave should keep its shape for a few seconds.

COOKING TIME
15
MINS

SERVES
10–12

PREP TIME
20
MINS

INGREDIENTS

75g dark chocolate, broken into chunks

4 large eggs

120g caster sugar, plus extra for sprinkling

30g plain flour

30g cocoa powder, plus a little extra for dusting

FOR THE CHOCOLATE FROSTING

70g butter

4 tbsp cocoa powder

3 tbsp Baileys

220g icing sugar, plus extra for dusting (optional)

4 Sift the flour and cocoa powder over the cake batter, add the cooled melted chocolate and gently fold them in until they are all fully incorporated. Pour the mixture into the tin, carefully level the surface and bake the cake for 14–15 minutes until it is just firm to the touch.

5 While the cake is baking, lay a sheet of baking parchment on a wire cooling rack and sprinkle a light dusting of cocoa powder over it. Take the cake out of the oven and turn it out of the tin on to the cocoa-coated parchment. Carefully peel off the parchment on the bottom of the sponge, then roll it up from one long edge and leave it to cool.

6 For the frosting, melt the butter in a medium pan over a low heat, add the cocoa powder and stir to combine the two. Remove the pan from the heat. In a small pan heat the Baileys, then add it to the chocolate mixture along with most of the icing sugar. Beat until the mixture is smooth and add the rest of the icing sugar if you need it. You should have a thick, spreadable frosting.

7 Unroll the sponge. It may crack a little but don't worry, the frosting will cover the cracks. Spread a third of the frosting over it, then roll it up again and place it on a serving plate, seam side down. Cut a quarter off the end of the cake at an angle and attach to the side of the cake with a little frosting. Spread the remaining icing all over the yule log, including the ends, and with a fork swirl in a pattern to resemble bark. Dust with a little icing sugar and add a robin or two and some trees on the side of the plate to create a Christmassy scene. Alternatively leave the roulade whole and smooth the icing to an even layer scatter over white chocolate stars and leave to set before cutting into slices to serve.

CONVERSION CHARTS

DRY WEIGHTS

GRAMS (G)	OUNCES (OZ)	GRAMS (G)	OUNCES (OZ)
5	¼	500	1LB 2OZ
8/10	⅓	550	1LB 3OZ
15	½	600	1LB 5OZ
20	¾	625	1LB 6OZ
25	1	650	1LB 7OZ
30/35	1¼	675	1½LB
40	1½	700	1LB 9OZ
50	2	750	1LB 10OZ
60/70	2½	800	1¾LB
75/85/90	3	850	1LB 14OZ
100	3½	900	2LB
110/120	4	950	2LB 2OZ
125/130	4½	1KG	2LB 3OZ
135/140/150	5	1.1KG	2LB 6OZ
170/175	6	1.25KG	2¾LB
200	7	1.3/1.4KG	3LB
225	8	1.5KG	3LB 5OZ
250	9	1.75/1.8KG	4LB
265	9½	2KG	4LB 4OZ
275	10	2.25KG	5LB
300	11	2.5KG	5½LB
325	11½	3KG	6½LB
350	12	3.5KG	7¾LB
375	13	4KG	8¾LB
400	14	4.5KG	9¾LB
425	15	6.8KG	15LB
450	1LB	9KG	20LB
475	1LB 1OZ		

LIQUID MEASURES

568ML = 1 UK PINT (20FL OZ) | 16FL OZ = 1 US PINT

METRIC (ML)	IMPERIAL (FL OZ)	CUPS
15	½	1 TBSP (LEVEL)
20	¾	
25	1	1/8
30	1¼	
50	2	¼
60	2½	
75	3	

100	3½	3/8
110/120	4	½
125	4½	
150	5	2/3
175	6	¾
200/215	7	
225	8	1
250	9	
275	9½	
300	½ PINT	1¼
350	12	1½
375	13	
400	14	
425	15	
450	16	2
500	18	2¼
550	19	
600	1 PINT	2½
700	1¼ PINTS	
750	11/3 PINTS	
800	1 PINT 9FL OZ	
850	1½ PINTS	
900	1 PINT 12FL OZ	3¾
1 LITRE	1¾ PINTS	1 QUART (4 CUPS)
1.2 LITRES	2 PINTS	1¼ QUARTS
1.25 LITRES	2¼ PINTS	
1.5 LITRES	2½ PINTS	3 US PINTS
1.75/1.8 LITRES	3 PINTS	
2 LITRES	3½ PINTS	2 QUARTS
2.2 LITRES	3¾ PINTS	
2.5 LITRES	41/3 PINTS	
3 LITRES	5 PINTS	
3.5 LITRES	6 PINTS	

OVEN TEMPERATURES

°C	°F	GAS MARK	DESCRIPTION
110	225	¼	COOL
130	250	½	COOL
140	275	1	VERY LOW
150	300	2	VERY LOW
160/170	325	3	LOW TO MODERATE
180	350	4	MODERATE
190	375	5	MODERATELY HOT
200	400	6	HOT
220	425	7	HOT
230	450	8	HOT
240	475	9	VERY HOT

INDEX

HarperCollins*Publishers*
1 London Bridge Street
London SE1 9GF

www.harpercollins.co.uk

HarperCollins*Publishers*
Macken House, 39/40 Mayor Street Upper,
Dublin 1, D01 C9W8
Ireland

First published by HarperCollins*Publishers*
2021

10 9 8 7 6 5 4

drinkaware.co.uk

A catalogue record of this book is available
from the British Library

ISBN 978-0-00-845498-2

Recipe writer: Jayne Cross
Photographer: Maja Smend
Food stylist: Jayne Cross
Prop stylist: Sarah Birks

Printed and bound in Latvia by PNB Print

MIX
Paper | Supporting
responsible forestry
FSC™ C007454

This book is produced from independently
certified FSC™ paper to ensure
responsible forest management.

For more information visit: www.
harpercollins.co.uk/green

WHEN USING KITCHEN
APPLIANCES PLEASE ALWAYS
FOLLOW THE MANUFACTURER'S
INSTRUCTIONS